Father Bombo's
Pilgrimage to Mecca

— *1770* —

By HUGH HENRY BRACKENRIDGE

and PHILIP FRENEAU

EDITED, WITH AN
INTRODUCTION, BY

MICHAEL DAVITT BELL

PRINCETON UNIVERSITY

LIBRARY

CONTENTS

ACKNOWLEDGMENTS

I should like to thank those at the Princeton University Library whose generous aid and assistance facilitated virtually every stage of the preparation of this edition: Gerald Eades Bentley, Mina R. Bryan, William S. Dix, Richard M. Ludwig and the staff of the University Archives. Constance K. Escher, of the Davis Center for Historical Studies, made available the files of the projected Dictionary of Alumni Biography. Henry Knight Miller, of the Princeton English Department, made numerous suggestions about the literary background of *Father Bombo's Pilgrimage*. Jan Lilly's design nicely captures the spirit of the original manuscript. And very special thanks are due to Dr. Howard T. and Pauline Behrman, who agreed to the publication of *Father Bombo's Pilgrimage* when it was part of their collection, and who later generously donated the manuscript to the Princeton University Library.

M. D. B.

INTRODUCTION

The honor of "first American novel" is usually given either to Thomas Atwood Digges' *Adventures of Alonso . . . By a Native of Maryland* (1775) or to Francis Hopkinson's *A Pretty Story* (1774).[1] But *Father Bombo's Pilgrimage to Mecca*, although published here for the first time in its entirety, was written in 1770, and might thus plausibly claim the distinction of chronological priority. It is also more properly a "novel" than *A Pretty Story*, which is a brief and straightforward political allegory. And it has, unlike Digges' *Adventures*, an American setting (in Book I and Chapter 1 of Book II). *Father Bombo's Pilgrimage* is an early work of two men who later came to rank among the most important literary figures of the American Revolution and early Republic. Hugh Henry Brackenridge (1748-1816), a distinguished Pennsylvania jurist and politician, was more widely known as the author of *Modern Chivalry* (1792-1815), the most substantial work of American social or political fiction before Cooper. Philip Freneau (1752-1832) rose to fame

---

[1] Digges' *Adventures* was first published in London, and is reprinted in facsimile, edited by Thomas J. MacMahon (New York: U. S. Catholic Historical Society, 1943), along with Robert H. Elias's article, "The First American Novel." Hopkinson's *A Pretty Story: Written in the Year of Our Lord 2774, by Peter Grievous, Esq. . . .* was first published in Philadelphia, 1774; a revised version appears in Hopkinson's *Miscellaneous Essays and Occasional Writings*, 3 vols. (Philadelphia, 1792). For a modern reprint see Walter C. Bronson, ed., *American Prose (1607-1865)* (Chicago: University of Chicago Press, 1916), pp. 183-197. Chronological priority might be claimed for Joseph Morgan's *The History of the Kingdom of Basaruah* (1715), reprinted in Richard Schlatter, ed., *The History of the Kingdom of Basaruah, and Three Unpublished Letters, by Joseph Morgan* (Cambridge: Harvard University Press, 1946). But Morgan's *History* is really a doctrinal religious allegory, with debts to Bunyan, rather than a novel. For a listing of American novels up to 1820, see Henri Petter, *The Early American Novel* (Columbus: Ohio State University Press, 1971), pp. 466-75.

(and in some circles infamy) as the author of anti-British satires during the Revolution, and as an anti-Federalist editor working for Jefferson in the early 1790's. Today he is even more valued for his lyrical nature poetry, which constitutes a milestone in America's movement from literary neo-classicism to Romanticism.[2]

These writers began their careers as members of the class of 1771 at the College of New Jersey at Nassau Hall (now Princeton University), where they were part of an extraordinary group of undergraduates. James Madison was a classmate, close friend and sometime collaborator in literary projects. Aaron Burr (whose father, also Aaron Burr, and grandfather, Jonathan Edwards, had both served in the Presidency of the New Jersey college) was a member of the class of 1772. Many other students of the time went on to distinguish themselves in the political, religious and literary life of the new nation.[3] It was here, in the

[2] The best biography of Brackenridge is Claude M. Newlin, *The Life and Writings of Hugh Henry Brackenridge* (Princeton: Princeton University Press, 1932). See also Martha Conner, "Hugh Henry Brackenridge at Princeton University, 1768-1771," *Western Pennsylvania Historical Magazine*, 10 (1927), 146-62. The fullest biographical and critical study of Freneau is Lewis Leary, *That Rascal Freneau: A Study in Literary Failure* (New Brunswick: Rutgers University Press, 1941). See also the introduction to Fred Lewis Pattee, ed., *The Poems of Philip Freneau, Poet of the American Revolution* (Princeton: Princeton University Library, 1902-1907), 3 vols., vol. 1, pp. xi-cxii.

[3] The best and most recent history of the College of New Jersey is Thomas Jefferson Wertenbaker, *Princeton, 1746-1896* (Princeton: Princeton University Press, 1946). Among earlier histories the most useful are John Maclean, *History of the College of New Jersey, From its Origin in 1746 to the Commencement of 1854* (Philadelphia: Lippincott, 1877), 2 vols.; and Samuel Davies Alexander, *Princeton College During the Eighteenth Century* (New York: A. D. F. Randolph, 1872). Except where otherwise noted information about particular students of the period has been gathered from the biographical files on alumni maintained by the Princeton University Archives (in Firestone Library, Princeton University) or—in the case of the best-known alumni—from the *Dictionary of American Biography*.

fall of 1770 when they were juniors, that Brackenridge and Freneau produced *Father Bombo's Pilgrimage*. The work is a piece of undergraduate humor, occasioned by the so-called "paper war" of 1770-71—a voluminous exchange of satires between the rival American Whig and Cliosophic literary societies which dominated undergraduate life in Princeton.[4] Brackenridge and Freneau had helped found the Whig Society, and the immediate purpose of their burlesque novel was to ridicule the Cliosophians.

Few documents of the paper war survive. Ashbel Green, a Whig of the class of 1783 and later President of the college, recalled in 1818 that during his undergraduate days "a considerable number of the pieces written by the Whigs was preserved and held in great estimation by the Society."[5] Unfortunately these manuscripts were lost in 1802 in a fire which gutted Nassau Hall, destroying almost all the early records of the college and the societies. This fire also presumably destroyed the original manuscript of *Father Bombo's Pilgrimage*. Until recently the only known trace of the novel has been a manuscript notebook in the hand of William Bradford, a member of the class of 1772, co-founder of the Whig Society and later Attorney General of the United States. The second half of Bradford's notebook contains his copy of a group of poems by Brackenridge, Freneau and Madison, entitled "Satires Against the Tories," and satirizing various members of the Cliosophic Society. These are preceded by Bradford's copy of only Book III of *Father Bombo's Pilgrimage*. Bradford's version of Book III *has* been published:

[4] On the histories of the two undergraduate literary societies see Charles Richard Williams, *The Cliosophic Society, Princeton University: A Study of its History in Commemoration of its Sesquicentennial Anniversary* (Princeton: Princeton University Press, 1916), and especially Jacob N. Beam, *The American Whig Society of Princeton University* (Princeton: American Whig Society, 1933).

[5] "History of the American Whig Society," quoted in Beam, *The American Whig Society*, p. 61.

Chapter I (by Brackenridge) in Newlin's *Life and Writings of Hugh Henry Brackenridge*, pp. 15-21; Chapters II and III and the Conclusion (all by Freneau), as edited by Lewis Leary, in *The Pennsylvania Magazine of History and Biography*, 66 (1942), 459-478.[6] Books I and II were supposed to have vanished.

In the 1950's, however, another manuscript notebook came to light, this one in the hand of John Blair Smith, a Whig of the class of 1773 and later first President of Union College (his brother, Samuel Stanhope Smith, was President of the College of New Jersey from 1795 to 1812). Smith's manuscript, dated from August 23 to September 13, 1772, was presumably, like Bradford's, copied from the lost Freneau-Brackenridge original preserved by the Whig Society until the fire of 1802. But unlike Bradford's, Smith's contains the text of the entire novel. Thus the present edition follows the Smith manuscript, recently donated to the Princeton University Library by Dr. Howard T. Behrman of New York City and Princeton.[7]

There has been no effort to collate Smith's version of Book III with Bradford's; there are too many variations (most of them minor), and the relative authority of the two manuscripts is unclear. It has seemed advisable, however, to make a few silent editorial corrections, especially in the case of errors which seem more likely to be Smith's than Brackenridge's or Freneau's. Smith's punctuation, eccentric and often capricious, has been altered where it clearly violates the syntax of the text. The future Presi-

[6] The Bradford Manuscript is currently in the collection of the Historical Society of Pennsylvania, at Philadelphia.

[7] The Smith manuscript was discovered in 1957 by Dr. and Mrs. Stanley Parks, of Lexington, Kentucky. Following their inquiries, directed to the Princeton University Library, it was identified by Professor Laurence B. Holland, currently of Johns Hopkins University. The manuscript remained in the possession of Dr. and Mrs. Parks until 1973, when it was purchased by Dr. Behrman, who later generously donated it to the Princeton University Library. The whereabouts of the manuscript notebook from 1772 to 1957, and the process by which it got to Kentucky, are unknown.

dent of Union College was not, as an undergraduate, a master of spelling; he seems, among other things, to have learned the "i before e except after c" rule backwards. Such obvious spelling errors have been corrected, but not quaint forms still current in the later eighteenth century. Smith's use of capital letters is also capricious; initial "j's" and "g's" are almost always capitalized in the manuscript. In the present edition capitals are retained only at the beginning of nouns. Finally, in a very few cases, words have been supplied in passages that do not otherwise make sense.

The Smith manuscript nowhere names the authors of *Father Bombo's Pilgrimage*, except for the enigmatic initials, "I. L." or "J. Γ.," entered at the end of each chapter. In the Bradford manuscript of Book III, however, Chapter One is attributed to Brackenridge by name, Chapters Two and Three and the Conclusion to Freneau. Coincidentally, in Smith's version of Book III, Chapter One is signed "I. L.," all the rest "J. Γ." One may assume with some security, then, that all the chapters in Books I and II signed "I. L." are by Brackenridge, all those signed "J. Γ." by Freneau. This assumption has been followed here, in the bracketed identifications of each attribution. But the editor must confess himself at a loss to understand why Smith, unlike Bradford, would have felt compelled to conceal the identities of the authors, unless this concealment was a feature of the original (for which Bradford could have compensated, in his own version, through close personal acquaintance with the authors at the time of the book's composition). The precise significance of the initials is also mysterious; although one might speculate, given the near identity of "I" and "J," that the "Γ" is in fact an upside-down "L," so that the two sets of initials may be intended as upside-down versions of each other.

Brackenridge and Freneau both entered Princeton, as sophomores, in 1768—their arrival coinciding with the accession of the

Rev. John Witherspoon, an eminent Scottish clergyman, to the Presidency of the college. They came from quite different backgrounds. Brackenridge was born in Scotland in 1748, moving with his family to York County, Pennsylvania at the age of five. Raised on a farm, he became a scholar largely through his own determined efforts—both to pursue the enticements of learning and to escape the drudgery of agriculture. When he entered the College of New Jersey at the relatively advanced age of 20 he had already been a teacher himself, at a boys' school, for three years. Freneau's path to Nassau Hall was more natural. The grandson of a French Protestant tradesman, André Fresneau, who had emigrated to New York in 1707, Philip was born in 1752. When he was ten his family moved to Mount Pleasant, an estate near Middleton Point, New Jersey, where Freneau took full advantage of private tutoring and an ample library. He entered New Jersey College "so well prepared that President Witherspoon is said to have sent a letter of congratulation to his mother."[8] Although separated by background, and by four years in age, Brackenridge and Freneau soon became fast friends, united by a common interest in the classics, and a profound love of literature in general.

The College of New Jersey had been founded in 1746 by a coalition of "New Light" Calvinists, sympathetic to the Great Awakening of the early 1740's, who wished to establish a training-ground for Evangelical ministers in the Middle Colonies. But it was never simply a seminary, having been established, as well, to provide general education for laymen. And in order to secure a New Jersey charter it was opened to young men of all religious persuasions. In 1756, after subsisting in temporary quarters in Elizabeth and New Brunswick, it was moved into Nassau Hall, at Princeton. The plans of the founders involved "courses in the classics, in divinity, in philosophy and in science comparable to those at Harvard and Yale, or the Scottish uni-

[8] Pattee, ed., *The Poems of Philip Freneau*, p. xv.

versities or the English dissenting academies. This was not to be another advanced grammar school . . . but an institution of full collegiate grade."[9] How fully these ambitions were realized is not clear. And one of the principal objects of satire in *Father Bombo's Pilgrimage* is the gap between academic pretense and actual ignorance, most notoriously in Bombo's examination for the position of schoolmaster in Book III, Chapter 2.

Influenced by the British dissenting academies the college trained students in English composition and rhetoric. As far as the abilities of the small teaching staff would permit, upperclassmen were introduced to science and mathematics—as well as logic and metaphysics. Theology was of course an important part of the course of study. But the basis of the curriculum, especially in the first two years, was classical. Training in Greek and Latin was, at least in theory, the major (sometimes the only) requirement for admission. Freshmen were "kept doggedly at Horace, Cicero's *Orations*, the Greek *Testament*, Lucian's *Dialogues*, and Xenophon's *Cyropaedia*"; they were expected to know, as well, Homer and Virgil ("four books of Virgil's *Aeneid* together with the *Bucolics* and *Georgics*").[10] The influence of this curriculum is clear in the chapter-epigraphs in *Father Bombo's Pilgrimage*, drawn predominantly from Horace, but also from Homer, Virgil, and even Anacreon (although "modern" literature is represented by Chaucer and Spenser).[11] Classical education, or the pretense to classical education, also figures prominently in the novel itself. Bombo frequently pretends to a false mastery of Latin and Greek. And his adventures are initiated by the public discovery of his effort to pass off as his own work a plagiarized translation from Lucian's *Dialogues*.

[9] Wertenbaker, *Princeton*, p. 20.   [10] *Ibid.*, p. 93.

[11] Most of the classical epigraphs are identified, at least by author and usually by work, in the text. Of the two modern epigraphs (both to Book II, Chapter 3), the lines from Chaucer are adapted from the *Nun's Priest's Tale*, while that attributed to Spenser does not, as far as the editor has been able to determine, appear in that author's works. Perhaps the passage is a hoax.

Although President Witherspoon did not much alter this basic curriculum, his effect on the fledgling college was profound. He accomplished a great deal toward securing its educational integrity and financial security. He also, not entirely intentionally, transformed its purpose, from that of mainly training ministers to that of "chiefly . . . training men for public life."[12] This transformation—attested to by the later careers of such undergraduates as Madison, Burr, Freneau, Brackenridge and Bradford—may have been as much a sign of the times as a result of the new President's influence. But it was, in any case, the central fact of the experience of this generation of Princeton students.

Many of them seem to have discovered, and not without some agony, that the ministerial role was no longer obvious or compelling. Madison stayed on for a year to study Hebrew, but then returned home to live in indecision until "finding himself" in the political excitement of the Revolution. Brackenridge was ordained, but turned first to teaching (his career prior to coming to Princeton), and suffered a prolonged illness (which may in fact have been something like what we would call a nervous breakdown) in his first year of absence from Princeton. He, too, moved into revolutionary activity; and following the war he formally abandoned the ministry for a legal and political career. Freneau never did "find himself," oscillating instead between poetry, political journalism, farming and several stints as a sea-captain. This sense of insecurity, of profound uncertainty about future professional identity, is crucial to an understanding of these young men who came of age in the stress and violence of the Revolution—that War for Independence which finally provided, for many of them, a feeling of new purpose and promise. It is also crucial to an understanding of *Father Bombo's Pilgrimage*, of the aimlessness, violence and excess that characterize its coarse humor.

[12] Wertenbaker, *Princeton*, p. 76.

"The Castle": Nassau Hall in 1764, engraving by Henry Dawkins after an original by William Tennant (Princeton University Library).

Mr Bombo's Pilgrimage to Mecca. Book the second.

Chapter 1st

— si propius stes —
————————— te capiat magis. Horace
—— the nearer you behold
—— the more it strikes you

———— A true story ————

Dear brethren!

By yt. time I had reached yt. suburbs of N. York
grey twilight had stretched her sable curtains o'er one half of yt.
globe, the droning beetles wheeled their flight & yt. drowsy tinklings of yt. steeple bells inclined yt. minds of yt. serious to sober
thought. I had determined to lodge in yt. streets as a way-faring
man, like yt. Moabite of old when he came to a city of Gilead, till
till I considered yt. dangerous tendency of yt. night air &
yt. noxious vapours arising from yt. water, for, if I remember
right Aristotle has a precept some share to this purpose
    Let every travling Wight } Before yt. vapour's have
    Avoid yt. damps of night } Sent him to his grave —
Accordingly I pushed up yt. main street to yt. sign of yt.
twelve pigeons, but seeing several persons walking in yt.
Piazza daubed with gold & yt. like ensigns of Pride, I found
it was a house of entertainment for persons of quality
& therefore to procure a lodging there was a task too great

Smith Manuscript of *Father Bombo's Pilgrimage*, page 38: the opening of Book II.

Father Bombo's Pilgrimage to Mecca.
Book the third

Preface to Book 3.

The Editors of this work think fit to acquaint
him or those who shall read this history, that we
designed to comprize ye whole in ye three present books; but several intervening circumstances concurring to hinder our prosecution
of our design at large, we have concluded in as
hasty a manner as possible, tho' perhaps, too abruptly, which defect we hope our readers (if we
have any) will pardon, as also some mistakes
both in Grammar & Stile, which insensibly crept
in as we proceeded along, this being ye first
draught, warm from ye brain, & it was impossible
to correct it, without more blotting & interlin-
ations, than we would willingly chuse to insert

September 5th 1772.   ΣΓ & 1. ∠
Nassau Hall   Mutato nomine
                Fabula de te narratur.
                Change but ye name
                the story's told of you

Smith Manuscript of *Father Bombo's Pilgrimage*, page 77: the authors' preface to Book III.
Gives good examples of enigmatic initialled signatures used throughout.
The date (lower left) refers to Smith's copy, not the original composition.
Such dates have been omitted in the present edition.

Hugh Henry Brackenridge,
oil portrait by Gilbert Stuart,
painted about 1810 (Courtesy of
the University of Pittsburgh).

Philip Freneau, engraving
by Frederick Halpin, after an
unknown original (reproduced
from *Poems Relating to the
American Revolution* [1865]).

Witherspoon also significantly transformed the dominant philosophy of Nassau Hall. At the time of his arrival, the Idealism of Bishop Berkeley was winning many converts among the abler students. "But," as President Maclean described it in his *History of the College of New Jersey*, "this did not long continue, and the common-sense view of things which was beginning to prevail in Scotland soon gained the ascendency here, under the guidance of the new President, and on the part of the students the doctrine of the idealists became a matter for jest rather than for serious debate."[13] Such a jest occurs in Book III, Chapter 2 of *Father Bombo's Pilgrimage*, in Bombo's affirmative answer to the question of his interviewer and prospective employer: "Do you really believe you are nothing but a meer shadow, an immaterial something?" (p. 86) But the triumph of Scottish Common-Sense Philosophy over Idealism was not merely a matter of abstract metaphysics. Idealism, as articulated not by Berkeley but by former President Edwards, had been crucial to the theology of the Great Awakening, which had in turn given birth to the College of New Jersey. Witherspoon's philosophical triumph may thus have been instrumental in eroding his students' sense of possible dedication to careers as Evangelical Calvinist ministers. It is worth noting that when small religious revivals erupted at the college in 1770 and 1772 Witherspoon was rumored to have opposed them.[14]

The late 1760's and early 1770's were not only, however, a time for insecurity, for the questioning of traditional roles and patterns of belief. This was also a period of great excitement, in part political. From 1765 on, undergraduates regularly registered their objections to the repressive actions of the British Parliament. Their patriotism was supported by President Witherspoon, who would later sign the *Declaration of Independence* and serve in the Continental Congress. In 1765, and again in

[13] Maclean, *History of the College of New Jersey*, I, p. 403.
[14] *Ibid.*, pp. 389-90.

1770, the students attended Commencement exercises in clothing of entirely American manufacture. In July of 1770 a letter from New York merchants to their counterparts in Philadelphia, urging non-compliance with the Non-Importation Agreement, was intercepted in Princeton and publicly burned in front of Nassau Hall. This spirit of patriotic protest led to the naming of the American Whig Society, and led its members to defame the rival Cliosophians (rather unfairly) as "Tories."[15] The same spirit lies behind "The Rising Glory of America," the 1771 Commencement poem composed by Brackenridge and Freneau and read by Brackenridge at the final exercises.[16]

But the excitement agitating undergraduate life in Princeton in 1770 was also more generally literary, as the apparently enormous volume of writings exchanged in the 1770-71 paper war would suggest. Literature, like politics, provided an outlet for the frustrations and uncertainties of undergraduates in a period of transition; and the study of literature lay at the core of their formal curriculum. This is the excitement that animates *Father Bombo's Pilgrimage*. The chapters set at Nassau Hall—Book I, Chapter 2; and Book I, Chapter 4 (consisting of the interpolated story of "Aliborah the Skipper")—are centrally concerned with the uses and misuses of literature, especially poetry.

[15] The name of the society was drawn from William Livingston's 1768 letters protesting threats of Episcopal establishment in the colonies and signed "The American Whig." (See Beam, *The American Whig Society*, p. 36.) Beam insists that the name "Tory" (in the "Satires") was simply a slur, having no actual reference to the politics of the Cliosophians, many of whom went on to distinguish themselves in the Revolution. (*Ibid.*, pp. 45-6.)

[16] The extent to which "The Rising Glory of America" indicates an early open avowal of "revolutionary" sentiments can be exaggerated if its publishing history is forgotten. Freneau's revised version (1775) is indeed explicitly revolutionary. But the version read by Brackenridge at the 1771 Commencement, and published in Philadelphia in 1772, viewed the "glory" of America as "rising" within the context of a unified British Empire.

And throughout the novel one finds burlesques of the literary forms most familiar to late-eighteenth-century undergraduates: the formal debate, which Witherspoon had instituted at the college (Book II, Chapter 3), the sermon (II, 4), the topical essay (III, 2: on "Luxury"), the Latin Epitaph (in the Conclusion) and, most notably, Freneau's various pastiches of lachrymose verse. Also, as the chapter-epigraphs from Homer and Virgil suggest, the novel as a whole was at least partially intended as an American (or Princetonian) mock-epic.

Two years after graduating, Madison recalled this undergraduate enthusiasm for literature in a letter to Bradford.

> I was afraid [he wrote] you would not easily have loosened your affection from the belles lettres. A delicate taste and warm imagination like yours must find it hard to give up such refined and exquisite enjoyments for the coarse and dry study of the law. . . . I myself used to have too great a hankering after those amusing studies. Poetry, wit, and criticism, romances, plays, &c., captivated me much; but I began to discover that they deserve but a small portion of a mortal's time, and that something more substantial, more durable, and more profitable, befits a riper age. It would be exceedingly improper for a laboring man to have nothing but flowers in his garden, or to determine to eat nothing but sweet meats and confections. Equally absurd would it be for a scholar and a man of business to make up his whole library with books of fancy, and feed his mind with nothing but such luscious performances.[17]

This letter expresses a conventional bias of the period against over-indulgence in literature, a bias re-inforced by Scottish Common-Sense Philosophy and well represented by Madison's own

[17] Gaillard Hunt, ed., *The Writings of James Madison* (New York: Putnam's, 1900-1910), vol. I, pp. 11-12.

abandonment of "amusing studies" for the "more substantial" and "more durable" rewards of a political career.[18] And it suggests the difficulties young men of the time had in taking literature seriously once they had left college.

Freneau and Brackenridge are remembered today because they *did* continue to devote themselves to literature after graduating. But they were not unaffected by the sentiments Madison expressed. In spite of his massive picaresque novel, *Modern Chivalry*, and a few earlier efforts in verse and drama, Brackenridge never thought of himself primarily as a literary man. Turning to the law after serving as a chaplain in the Revolution, he became actively involved in Western Pennsylvania politics, in 1799 earning appointment to the Pennsylvania Supreme Court. Even *Modern Chivalry* was not a literary indulgence but an effort to discipline literature to the more serious purposes of political and moral instruction.

Freneau could not so easily subordinate his literary inclinations to the practical responsibilities of a "riper age." An opportunity to do so was offered by political satire, the mode with which he rapidly became identified; but he never found this mode entirely satisfactory. Even his earliest satires, including his contributions to *Father Bombo*, reveal a deeper impulse to find poetry and purpose not in political engagement but in the serenities of nature and of a purely poetic vocation.[19] In 1775

---

[18] Suspicion of fiction and imagination in early America is discussed in William Charvat, *The Origins of American Critical Thought, 1810-1835* (Philadelphia: University of Pennsylvania Press, 1936) and G. Harrison Orians, "Censure of Fiction in American Romances and Magazines, 1789-1810," *PMLA*, 52 (1937), 195-214. The relationship of this suspicion to Scottish ethical realism is the subject of Terence Martin, *The Instructed Vision: Scottish Common Sense Philosophy and the Origins of American Fiction* (Bloomington, Ind.: University of Indiana Press, 1961).

[19] For instance in "A Satire" (written in 1775, re-published as "Mac-Swiggen" in 1786) Freneau interpolates into the denunciation of his antagonist the following paean to nature and poetic escape: "O waft me far, ye muses of the west—/Give me your green bowers and soft seats of rest—/

this impulse drove him from the impending Revolution to the tranquility of the island of Santa Cruz, where he agonized over his divided obligations in one of his best early poems, "The Beauties of Santa Cruz," written in the politically significant year of 1776. Finding in this Danish colony an image of the plight of his homeland he imagined for himself not revolutionary commitment but poetic escape:

> What, though we bend to a tyrannic crown;
> Still Nature's charms in varied beauty shine—
> What though we own the rude imperious Dane,
> Gold is his sordid care, the Muses mine.[20]

So much for Madison's insistence on the "more profitable" concerns of maturity! The impulse to withdraw, both from politics and from the demands of practical maturity, is even clearer in the closing lines of the poem, addressed to his countrymen in the midst of their crisis:

> Still there remain—thy native air enjoy,
> Repell the tyrant who thy peace invades,
> While, pleas'd, I trace the vales of Santa Cruz
> And sing with rapture her inspiring shades.[21]

Freneau returned two years later to embrace the cause he here rejected, but it was an uneasy commitment. From 1778 on, his poetry alternated between "fancy" and satire, Nature and politics, as he himself alternated between poetic escape and practical commitment. Thus between 1784 and 1790 the "Poet of the American Revolution," as he was called, fled the pressures of post-war political controversy by going to sea, only to return to the center of this controversy as editor, from 1791 to 1793, of

---

Thrice happy in those dear retreats to find/A safe retirement from all human kind." (Pattee, ed., *The Poems of Philip Freneau*, vol. I, p. 208.)

[20] Pattee, ed., *The Poems of Philip Freneau*, vol. I, p. 267.

[21] *Ibid.*, p. 268.

the Jeffersonian *National Gazette*. Yet this second political career was as short-lived as the first; and alternation between engagement and retreat remained the pattern of Freneau's life. He was able neither to succeed in a practical career nor to follow consistently his more poetic inclinations. It remained for later generations of American writers to make "delicate taste and warm imagination" respectable as the basis of a mature vocation.

But *Father Bombo's Pilgrimage* was written in college, at a time when it was still permissible to indulge the "amusing studies" of literature, to hope that the pursuit of letters might provide a sense of purpose or stability generally lacking at Princeton in the 1760's and '70's. In this light the book is especially fascinating for the almost manic abandon with which it burlesques the literary traditions its authors most admired, and the literary forms with which they would soon become identified—the picaresque novel and the lyric poem. It is, for the most part, an indulgence, an extravagance, a sport.

Its immediate occasion was, as has been mentioned, the paper war of 1770-71. By 1770 literary societies or clubs had long been a fixture of college life at Princeton, and the rivalry between them became at times so intense that in 1769, for instance, two such societies were suppressed by the faculty. In the summer of 1769 a small band of sophomores, led apparently by Brackenridge, Freneau and Madison, formed a new club, the American Whig Society. In the following year another group from the next sophomore class formed the Cliosophic Society. And almost immediately the spirit of rivalry came once again to the fore, in the form of a voluminous exchange of satires by members of each society on the alleged poetic ineptitude, moral depravity, dishonesty, stupidity and even physical deformity of the members of the rival group. There would appear to have been little real content, little genuine animosity, behind this paper war. It was, rather, an affectation, something to do, a release from the insecurity or boredom of being an undergraduate in 1770.

Father Bombo's Pilgrimage is very much a part of this exchange. Indeed the newly discovered first book would seem to be virtually a *roman à clef*. Many of its incidents are apparently thinly-fictionalized accounts, from the Whig point of view, of incidents in the paper war, and many of its characters correspond to actual members of the two societies, although most of these specific references remain obscure to the modern reader. In this light the immediate object of the novel is identical with that of the poetic "Satires Against the Tories" and the other, lost documents of the literary battle: to defame by any means, fair if necessary but foul wherever possible, the principal champions of the rival society.

Bombo's adventures begin at the "ancient and venerable castle" which a footnote in the Smith manuscript identifies as "New Jersey college." (page 3)[22] His first adventure stems from a quarrel between "two mighty Heroes," identified in a note as "H. Brackenridge and S. Spring who for diversion fought a pretended duel in the lower entry." (page 4) Brackenridge, to whom Bombo assigns the victory, was of course one of the principal Whigs involved in the paper war. Samuel Spring, a native of Uxbridge, Massachusetts, was a member of the class of 1771 who went on to become a conservative Congregational minister in Newburyport and one of the founders of Andover Theological Seminary. From the "Satires Against the Tories," in which the Cliosophians are attacked by name, it is clear that at Princeton he was one of their main literary champions. The "Satires" also

[22] The authority of the notes is unclear. They may have existed in the Freneau-Brackenridge original. They may have been inserted by Smith. Or they may have been added to the original by other Whigs during the two years between the composition of the novel and Smith's copying of it, to preserve the memory of events unknown to new undergraduates who entered the college after 1770.

inform us that "Spring wrote an absurd piece called the skipper—without sense or connection."[23] Thus he also lies behind the character Aliborah the Skipper, in *Father Bombo*, who tells his tale (presumably another fictionalized version of an incident in the paper war) in Book I, Chapter 4—and who sails with Bombo on Commodore Russel's ship in Book II, Chapter 3.

It is more difficult, and in most cases impossible, to identify the other characters in the novel. A few Cliosophians are given their own names. At the close Bombo leaves his effects "to his friends and Executors Mr. John Smith of N. England and Mr. Joshua Hart, both residing in the castle." (page 95) The Latin epitaph on his tomb is attributed to "his learned and ingenious friend and countryman Mr. Nathan Perkins." (page 96) As Jacob Beam has pointed out, "Joshua Hart, John Smith, and Nathan Perkins were all of the Class of 1770 and were among those Seniors who were present at the foundation meeting of the Cliosophic Society on June 7, 1770."[24] Commodore Russel, with whom Bombo sails to Europe, may be Caleb Russel, another member of the class of 1770, a native of Long Island who later became Principal of the Morris Academy in Morristown, New Jersey. Emir Finley, the "Turkish Bashaw" from whom Bombo purchases his boots at the beginning of Book I, Chapter 2, may be Ebeneezer Finley (son of Samuel Finley, former President of the College) who died in 1790 after serving in the Revolution and moving to Ohio. These were the only students with these names at New Jersey College in 1770. But there is no other evidence to link them with the Cliosophic Society.

Even the identity of Father Bombo remains mysterious and

[23] Bradford MS, quoted by permission of the Historical Society of Pennsylvania. Spring is a major figure, often the protagonist, in many of Brackenridge's contributions to the "Satires." A note to one of Madison's contributions, "The aeriel Journey of the poet Laureate of the Cliosophic Society," identifies the "poet Laureate" as "Spring."

[24] Beam, *The American Whig Society*, p. 45.

conjectural. That he *was* intended to represent a particular Cliosophian is suggested pretty clearly by the last note in Smith's manuscript, which states that Bombo "was a student in the University." (page 23) Internal evidence, when combined with what little we know about the students at Princeton at the time, suggests three or four possible sources for Bombo, but does not make the case for any one of them fully persuasive. Bombo's pilgrimage begins with the discovery of his plagiarism of a translation from Lucian's *Dialogues*. This tale of plagiarism probably refers to an episode in the paper war, although no other record of such an episode survives. It may be significant that William Paterson of the class of 1763—future State Governor and namesake of Paterson, New Jersey—had translated two of Lucian's *Dialogues* for public presentation in 1760. After graduating he practiced law near Princeton, was frequently at the college in 1770 and appears to have acted as the principal patron of the new Cliosophic Society.[25] Thus an argument could be made for identifying him with Bombo. But this possibility is extremely remote; Lucian, after all, was a standard part of the college curriculum. If any reference to Paterson's translations is intended in *Father Bombo*, it seems most likely that they may have been the source of a later plagiarism by an undergraduate Cliosophian, to which Bombo's misadventure alludes.

Parts of the "Satires Against the Tories" suggest a more likely candidate for the identity of Father Bombo. One of the principal victims of the "Satires" is a Cliosophian of the class of 1772 named Samuel Eusebius McCorkle, who was born in Pennsylvania in 1746 and moved to North Carolina with his family ten year later. After graduating from Princeton he returned to North Carolina, where he founded the Zion-Parnassus classical school in 1785, and where he was instrumental in establishing the Uni-

[25] *Ibid.*, p. 39. Beam notes further that the name of the Cliosophic Society was probably taken from Paterson's *Cliosophic Oration*, delivered at the 1763 Commencement.

versity of North Carolina.[26] What makes him interesting here is the similarity between the descriptions of him in the "Satires" and the descriptions of Father Bombo in the Freneau-Brackenridge novel. Like Bombo he is portrayed as being large and pugnacious: Goliath, writes Brackenridge in "The Origin of the Tories," was "large as McOrkle and perhaps as strong." More important is McCorkle's most prominent characteristic: "Your beard is red," proclaims Freneau in one of the "Satires," "and swine like is your nose./Like burning bush your bushy head of hair." McCorkle himself is made to complain, in a poem by Brackenridge: "What tho' my nose and bristly hair is red/And like a forest shade [sic] my sun-like head."[27] One is thus tempted to see a reference to McCorkle in Bombo's physical transformation at the hands of Nadir Gaw, the barber, who singes his beard "as red as a fox." (page 9)

Unfortunately Bombo is not a native of North Carolina. In Book I, Chapter 6 he returns to his father's "palace" on Long Island. Only two of the students at Nassau Hall in 1770 are known to have come from Long Island. One is Caleb Russel, already suggested as the possible source of Commodore Russel. The other is Joshua Hart, identified in Freneau's "Conclusion" as one of Bombo's executors.[28] Of these two, Hart—who later returned to his native Long Island as a Presbyterian minister— seems the most plausible source for Bombo. Unlike Russel he was clearly associated with the Cliosophic Society, having attended the foundation meeting in 1770, and having belonged to

[26] For further information on McCorkle see James F. Hurly and Julia Goode Eagan, *The Prophet of Zion-Parnassus* (Salisbury, N. C., 1934).

[27] Bradford MS, quoted by permission of the Historical Society of Pennsylvania.

[28] Peter Fish, a member of the class of 1774, was also a native of Long Island. But the earliest date he could have entered the college would have been following the September, 1770 commencement, after the composition of *Father Bombo*. Also, although Fish is known to have been a member of the Cliosophic Society, he did not join until 1772.

the suppressed Well Meaning Club, Clio's lineal predecessor, since 1768.[29] Of particular interest is the fact that he came to college quite late in life: born in 1738, he would have been 32 at the time of his graduation in 1770. His age would thus explain the otherwise puzzling designation, "*Father* Bombo." It might be argued against Hart that he does not appear in the "Satires Against the Tories," and could not therefore have been very prominent in the paper war. But the "Satires" (unlike *Father Bombo's Pilgrimage*) were pretty clearly written during the 1770-71 academic year, *after* Hart's graduation in September.[30] Thus Joshua Hart, in spite of the physical resemblance between Bombo and the McCorkle of the "Satires," and although we know practically nothing about his personality or activities as an undergraduate, seems the most probable source for the narrator and anti-hero of *Father Bombo's Pilgrimage*.

In any case, whatever the specific identities of its characters, *Father Bombo's Pilgrimage* was initially inspired by the beginnings of the paper war between the Whig and Cliosophic Societies. But it was more generally inspired by the literary excitement which lay behind the formation of these societies. With the formal college curriculum dominated by the classics the societies provided a forum for the discussion of modern literature, and their libraries made many works of this literature available to members.[31] The influence of this reading is clear throughout

[29] See *Catalogue of the Cliosophic Society* . . . (Princeton: Cliosophic Society, 1886), p. 6.

[30] Since two of the lampooned Cliosophians, John Philips and John Warford, were members of the class of 1774, and would not, therefore, have entered the college until the fall of 1770 (following the September commencement) it is possible to date the "Satires" as having been written after September.

[31] The societies and their libraries clearly served this function in the early nineteenth century. Unfortunately all records of the contents of the society libraries in the eighteenth century were destroyed in the Nassau Hall fire

Father Bombo's Pilgrimage. Lewis Leary finds in Book III "something of Don Quixote and a little of Lemuel Gulliver."[32] In addition to Cervantes and Swift one might cite, as influences on the novel, Rabelais, Smollett, Sterne and Fielding. Bombo's combination of pugnacity and professed erudition particularly recalls Fielding's Parson Adams, in *Joseph Andrews.* But the most obvious debt of the young American authors is revealed in the basic plot of their novel; for in sending their hero to Mecca, dressed in the supposed costume of a "devout musselman," they were clearly drawing on the vogue of oriental and pseudo-oriental fiction that swept England following the translation of the *Arabian Nights* between 1704 and 1712.

The oriental tale in England manifested itself in three main forms.[33] One, well exemplified by the *Arabian Nights* and subsequent imitations, was the tale of exotic adventure for its own sake, emphasizing the romance of strange customs and settings. There was also a strong tendency in England, most notable in Samuel Johnson's *Rasselas* (1759), to adapt Eastern customs and settings to the purposes of generalized moral allegory. Finally, the translation of Giovanni Paolo Marona's *Turkish Spy* (1687-93) and of Montesquieu's *Persian Letters* (1730) gave currency to a satirical variant of the oriental tale: the collection of letters, by a supposed Eastern visitor, commenting on the peculiarities of Western society. The best-known English example of satirical oriental fiction was Oliver Goldsmith's *Citizen of the World* (1762), and the mode gained considerable currency in America, most notably in the letters of Mustapha Rub-a-dub Keli Khan in

---

of 1802. Still, one may assume that these libraries, even in the eighteenth century, contained at least a representative selection of the major works of "modern" literature.

[32] Leary, *That Rascal Freneau*, p. 25.

[33] See Martha Pike Conant, *The Oriental Tale in England in the Eighteenth Century* (New York: Columbia University Press, 1908).

the *Salmagundi* papers (1807) of Washington Irving, William Irving and James Kirke Paulding.

Yet *Father Bombo's Pilgrimage* does not conform at all closely to any of these modes current in English oriental fiction. It is clearly not a moral allegory on the model of *Rasselas*. And while Fred Lewis Pattee could write of Bombo's adventures in Book III that they "read like chapters from the 'Arabian Nights,' "[34] even here the similarity is not very deep. Bombo does not reach Arabia itself until the final chapter, where his adventures are described in an extremely perfunctory manner. The climactic visit to Mecca occupies only two pages. Most of Bombo's "oriental" adventures actually take place in a very non-exotic America—an America to which Bombo tries, without much success, to attribute the romance of Arabia.

In fact the novel's veneer of orientalism is quite thin, being mainly a matter of costumes and names. Bombo wears a turban, carries a copy of the Koran (or "Alcoran"), calls inns "Caravanseries" and encounters characters with such pseudo-Arabian names as Nadir Gaw, Aliborah, or Solyman Houli Hhan (although the latter has an unsettling Irish ring to it). One might compare Bombo to the visiting foreigner of the oriental satire tradition, viewing Western customs through an outsider's eye. But Bombo's "oriental" perspective (like the "oriental" setting through which he moves) is bogus. And the contrast between East and West, between Bombo's exotic mission and the mundane world in which he travels, is by and large not satirical but simply humorous. The placing of an Arabian barber in Princeton, or of a turban on Bombo's head, is a joke, a juxtaposition of incongruous elements; but the joke has no discernable satirical import beyond general mockery—of the Cliosophians, of the American setting, of the tradition of oriental romance. All of this is to say that *Father Bombo's Pilgrimage* is less a satire than a

[34] Pattee, ed., *The Poems of Philip Freneau*, p. xviii.

burlesque, an effort to "make fun" of everything within the authors' purview.

The novel's humor is distinguished by a kind of vigorous aimlessness, an air of exuberant excess masking a profound uncertainty of general attitude. Literary clichés are mocked throughout, but the book has no language of its own. While drawing on a host of sources, it does so only superficially, and always in the form of burlesque. Its mockery of institutions and behavior is not supported by any norm, any imagined set of alternative values. Its world is one, finally, of relativity, in which *everything* becomes the object of mockery and parody. One curious result of this universal air of mockery is that Father Bombo himself, who begins as an object of ironic satire, becomes by the end almost a genuine hero—at least the sort of hero suited to a world which seems to *require* mendacity, buffoonery, self-absorption and physical durability for survival. For there is, in this world, no ultimate standard of literary or moral authority. All standards and values are fair game for the authors' humor.

The absence of value in *Father Bombo*—what one might call, less charitably, its moral and aesthetic incoherence, its pervasive air of adolescence—no doubt owes much to the immaturity and inexperience of its authors. One cannot expect too much of the "first American novel." But the very faults of the book provide much of its historical interest. It is the product, after all, of a period of rapid transition and uncertainty in American culture— qualities particularly crucial to the experience of undergraduates at the College of New Jersey. Old traditions of authority—personal, literary and political—were being profoundly challenged. New sources of legitimacy had not yet been tested. It is small wonder that such a climate should produce a work like *Father Bombo's Pilgrimage*. In its most adolescent qualities it seems most indicative of its milieu and moment.

These same qualities forge the most significant link between *Father Bombo* and the subsequent development of American literature. Humor has lain behind many of the works of our major writers, and it has often been characterized by generalized mockery, uncertainty of value and near or total moral incoherence. One thinks of some of the works of Mark Twain—particularly *A Connecticut Yankee*, in which satirical impulses war continually with moral confusion and the impulse to the joke, however grotesque or inappropriate. Even closer to Freneau and Brackenridge is the humor of the young Washington Irving (especially in *Salmagundi*) in which, as William Hedges has written, attempts at satire are accompanied by "no sure sense of authority." Lacking such a sense, and unable otherwise to find coherence in its world, as Hedges writes, "*Salmagundi* pushes the tendency of self-mockery to the point of explicitly defying its readers to make sense of the contents."[35] This is not to imply that *Father Bombo's Pilgrimage* is by any standard on the same aesthetic level as the works of Irving or Twain; it most assuredly is not. Yet it suggests, nevertheless, some of the directions in which American fiction would go following the Revolution. And its protagonist suggests the effect humor and social instability would have on our perception of the American character. Bombo may be based, strictly speaking, on Joshua Hart or some other Cliosophian; and he may occasionally resemble Don Quixote, Roderick Random or Parson Adams. But one finds in him, as well, fascinating hints of such later American anti-heroes as Ichabod Crane, Simon Suggs or even Huckleberry Finn.

Father Bombo's Pilgrimage to Mecca is hardly a neglected masterpiece. In most respects it falls short of the minimal standards of "good" fiction. Its coarse humor is far from suggesting the "refined and exquisite" literary enjoyments Madison recalled so wistfully in 1774. Yet the book is fascinating for several reasons. It *is* quite plausibly the "first American novel." Its authors became, later, important American writers. It gives a sense of the

---

[35] *Washington Irving: An American Study, 1802–1832* (Baltimore: Johns Hopkins University Press, 1965), pp. 26, 45.

fictional models and modes to which young Americans turned before the ascendency of Sentimental and Gothic influence in the
works of William Hill Brown, Susannah Haswell Rowson,
Charles Brockden Brown and their contemporaries—or before
the later domestication of historical romance by James Fenimore
Cooper and the many American adulators of Sir Walter Scott.
It suggests some of the directions American humor would take
in the next century. And it is especially fascinating as a document
of an aspect of American culture for which few such documents
exist—namely, the intellectual history of that generation of college students who later comprised the political and cultural elite
of the new nation. For all these reasons it is good, after a gap of
two centuries, to have the full text of the novel.

Michael Davitt Bell
Williams College

Father Bombo's Pilgrimage to Mecca

Wherein is given a true and faithful account
of the occasion of his journey and the
innumerable ills and disasters which befell him
in the course of his travels, 'till he returned
once more to his native country.

Hic Labor extremus.

VIRGIL BOOK 3ᵈ v. 714

Book the First

Favete Linguis.

HOR: LIB. 3. ODE 1.

Chapter 1st

Containing Mr. Bombo's first harangue to his brethren after his return from his Pilgrimage.

He assembled them in a Hall in the castle so often mentioned in this Book and spoke thus:

Worthy Brethren,

Perhaps many of you may wonder at the strange inducement that first led me to set out from my native land on that long and dangerous Pilgrimage which I have just finished; and forasmuch as several persons have maliciously reported that I was not quite sound in my mental Faculties, I have been prevailed upon by some of my intimate Friends, to relate the whole affair with my own mouth, from first to last after my departure from this ancient and venerable castle,* neither advancing nor retrenching from the real truth, relating each circumstance faithfully without any exaggeration. So help me Mahomet.

Many of you, my brethren, well know that I lived in great peace and harmony for many years in this antique and famous castle, which you also know is a paternal inheritance delivered down from father to son through several generations, and at present possessed by us their worthy descendants: here, brethren, I need not tell you, I employed my leisure hours in profitable and useful studies, such as Mathematics, Philosophy, Logic and the other branches of polite learning. I also frequently dipped into the sublime and pleasing scenes of Poetry in which I may tell you without vanity I made a most surprizing progress, my Odes ran as smooth as those of Horace and, some say, equalled the fire and rapidity of Pindar. Thus, you have a slight notion in which I passed my time, 'till the fatal year 1769, a year that I shall for the future insert in the fools Calendar, and the name of which I shall never mention without a sigh; the day in particular that ushered me forth into the ocean of my troubles, was the Sat-

* New Jersey college.

urday before Christmas: that day put an end to my felicity and plunged me into a gulph of misfortunes the various causes and reasons of which, worthy brethren, I am now to display.

Some months before this unhappy day two mighty Heroes* arrived at our castle from distant countries, in order to sojourn with us, proving their right and title by virtue of an ancient writing, wherein it was shown by indisputable Evidence, that their ancestors had a share in building this castle and consequently had a right to inhabit it. Long had not these valiant chiefs lived here before an unlucky Quarrel broke out between them, which rose to so great a height that they resolved to decide the dispute by sword and pistol; they accordingly fought and some say one of them had his ribs sorely scraped by a bullet and was quickly vanquished,* others say he had only a slight wound on the arm; but let this be as it will, it seems he was vanquished and indeed I make no wonder of it, as some people have told me he was very indifferently skilled in the use of arms both offensive and defensive, that are commonly used in duelling. However after these worthies had compromised the difference between them, I undertook to write an heroic poem in their honour; this, after mature deliberation I concluded to write in blank verse; which, to make short of the story, I finished in less than a month, and between us be it said, brethren, an excellent poem it was unless I am wofully deceived, for I imitated my great master Blackmore with all my power, tho' some evil-minded persons have insinuated, that I neither equalled him in grandeur of thought nor bombastical expressions; I shall not attempt to prove any thing to the contrary, which I might very easily do, and I dare say to your satisfaction, were I not obliged to proceed as the nature of my history directeth. After I had finished this poem and corrected it with my own hand with the greatest care and accuracy and

* H. Brackenridge and S. Spring who for diversion fought a pretended duel in the lower entry.
* Sam. Spring.

wrote it in the neatest manner, I presented it to the victorious chief.* I leave you to judge, how I was surprized, when upon presenting it to him, instead of receiving at least an hundred guineas as I expected, he being in a very angry mood after reading two or three lines gave a furious stamp with his foot and immediately tore it to pieces and threw it into the fire, but this was only smoke; the fire was yet to come. "Damn you, you little rascal," said he, "were you not beneath my notice I would this instant hack that woolly head of yours off its confounded stump and leave you a prey to the rats and mice in the garret. What do you mean by plaguing me with your Grub-street nonsense? Begone this moment from my presence or I'll make you an example to all who dare insult me." This he uttered in a menacing tone and with a most furious countenance, and I verily believe he would have put his threats in execution, (for his broad sword† was half drawn ready to smite me to the earth) had I not begged my life in the most moving manner and found favour, tho' by Mahomet! I did not get off without half a dozen kicks on the breech, which, as they were not bestowed in a very mild manner, sent me head long into the open Entry in a wretched plight much bruised and battered, my posteriors in particular were almost pounded to mummy and in a mournful condition. I made shift however to crawl away pensive and ashamed to my own apartment lamenting my ill fortune, but comforting myself at certain intervals, with that sentence out of Horace, "Nil desperandum est." I at length reached my chamber full of melancholy thoughts and sad reflections, where I considered the various evils which attend the good in this life and the success of the evil part of mankind. Moreover notwithstanding this rebuff here it was I first conceived the design of writing a Dialogue* between these Heroes, in revenge for the ill usage I received at their hands. I

* H. Brackenridge.   † Brackenridge was a Scotchman.
* Such a dialogue was actually wrote, of which our pilgrim was supposed to be the author or rather thief, as it was wholly almost stolen from Lucian.

represented them, travelling thro' the infernal regions, commonly called Hell, conversing with Charon and the ghosts of wicked men, sailing in the Stygian ferry boat, and many other droll things of the same kind equally harmonious and entertaining. To make short of the matter the piece was published and received with great applause, but here a second confounded misfortune befell me, which in brief was this: I had an ancient manuscript in my chamber wrote in Greek called, if I mistake not, Lucian's Dialogues; from this manuscript I took the hint of my dialogue and indeed to tell the truth stole it altogether except a word here and there of my own, but unluckily for me there chanced to be in the Castle another manuscript of the same kind, and as it was word for word the same with my own, the cheat was detected and universally laughed at. But this was by no means the period of my misfortunes. For at the dead of night when men forget their cares and departed Ghosts walk over the tombs of the dead and haunt the doleful solitude of a country church-yard, I heard a terrible scratching at my door with most dreadful yells and screams so that I thought all the Devils in hell were coming to carry me off without benefit of clergy; at last a pale, dim light shone thro' the crannies of my room when suddenly entered the Ghost of the great Apostate Lucian; I knew him by his long white beard and furious countenance, but while I was eying him he look'd sternly in my face and uttered these terrible words, "O thou wretched rascal Bombo, how didst thou dare to disturb my Ghost by first stealing and then retailing to the world my writings that were ever admired among men where they have been read; be assured for this thou shalt do penance with the utmost rigour and shalt suffer for thine own folly; but I must retire, the inexorable Pluto recalls me to his hateful kingdom. In less than an hour thou shalt be informed what labours thou art to undergo in doing penance for this crime." Scarce had he finished these words when the Clock struck twelve, he vanished, the dim light ceased to shine and all was silent as before; I lay shuddering in expectation of what was to happen in an hour. The clock at last struck one, when the shade of the famous prophet Mahomet rose through the floor and drew the curtains of my bed. I knew him by his Turban and Turkish vest. What, said I, with inexpressible anguish, am I to be tormented this night with all the imps of Orcus, or all the furies, snakes, Harpies, three-headed dogs and Devils that ever hell produced. Scarce was this fled from my jaws when the Turk in a furious tone spoke thus: "Impious wretch, know that I am come from the banks of Styx and the muddy shores of the infernal rivers whose slow moving waters wind in perpetual mases thro' the silent land of shades. A complaint of a most heinous nature has been made to me by the Ghost of Lucian charging you with the crime of Plagiarism, by publishing as your own what he wrote several hundred years ago. Know then that for this I command thee to take a long and tedious Journey to Mecca the sacred city of my nativity, but first thou art required to change thy religion and profess Mahometanism and become a zealous musselman. Thou art also hereby commanded to conform thy dress to the Turkish habit and particularly that of a Pilgrim and moreover thou art charged and strictly ordered to take some present suitable to the occasion to deposit in one of the Arabian Mosques that thou mayst atone for thy folly and appease the injured Ghost of Lucian." So saying he vanished away and soon after the morning dawned and I began to put in execution all he had commanded me, preparing for my destined journey and equipping myself in the best manner possible. But this shall be the subject of my next chapter.

JΓ
[Philip Freneau]

Chapter 2^d

Non eget Mauris jaculis neque Arcu.
HOR. BOOK 1st ODE 22

The holy prophet inspired me with resolutions stronger and stronger to prosecute my intended journey. I reflected on the decay in grandeur of all things here below, the ruins of Rome, the troubles of good men in this world and the punishments of the bad in the next. When I thought how long and dangerous the Journey was to Mecca and the holy land I was sorely distressed, but when I recollected that the aims of a penitent Pilgrim could subvert the stratagems of the wicked I was emboldened to proceed. My aspect was gloomy and my skin ill-favoured by intense studying of occult sciences. However after I had bathed myself nine times in a laver of Castilian soap my countenance became fairer than that of a Sultanness; I cloathed myself in a Turkish vest and bound it with a rope of straw. Tho' it was customary for Pilgrims to travel bare-footed yet I prayed to Mahomet to indulge his servant the liberty of a pair of jack-boots; it was accordingly granted and I borrowed a large pair from a Turkish Bashaw, the conductor of a Caravan, then going to Mecca, whose name was Emir Finley. Having drawn on my jack-boots I went to the apartments of my friends and gave them a full account of my resolution and cause of my intended journey. Tears gushed from their eyes. But permit me to pass in silence the tender scene which then ensued; we shook hands and with a sorrowful countenance I departed full of pious Meditations. I walked forth by the way of the old wall and came into the main-street which led me to the shop of Nadir Gaw the barber. Nadir treated me with great civility and applauded my resolution of atoning for my sins; he shaved my head and upper lip and earnestly intreated me to let him diminish my beard by the length of a span or raise it into curls to my chin, declaring, as he never expected to see me again he would powder it at his own Expense. Nadir, said I, I am an intended Pilgrim and a frizzled and powdered beard agree not to the humility of the true penitent; suffer me then to retain my whiskers and persevere in my pious resolutions. Vile Miscreant, said he, thy beard shall be done off in the fashion; saying that he snatched a red hot iron from the fire and singed my beard as red as a fox for which I shall never forgive him. I stepped thence into the shop of Mr. Halsey the merchant and desired him to show me his finest linen; he handed down several, I chose one of 17 Ells for which I paid two pieces of gold. I bade him farewell and went to Boabdella the sultan's Taylor. Boabdella Riman, said I, let these 17 Ells be made into a Turban. In the mean Time I walked in the yard before his door seriously meditating and humming to myself the song of other times composed by me in the castle. Boabdella in the mean time signified to me that the Turban was compleated, I stepped in, he fitted it upon my head, I shook hands and Boabdella sighed, his wife wept and Tears flowed from my own Eyes. I walked thence by the back alley to the stall of Hassan Bashang the cobbler. Hassan, said I, make me a leathern pouch to carry my provisions in. As Mahomet is a prophet, said Hassan, what mean you father Bombo? I am bent, said I, on a pilgrimage to the holy land to atone for my sins. The cobbler applauded my intention and made me the pouch containing about two Gallons. The kind creature bestowed the making upon me and gave his blessing into the bargain. I departed thence with my Turban nodding like the spire of a steeple, and my boots reaching to the waist band of my breeches. I was now forty years of age, my legs were swollen with the gout and the sedentary life I led in the castle, my belly was prominent and hung out like a Corporal's drum. I wanted nothing now to compleat my walking equipage except a staff which I also procured from Houli Cuff a negro slave belonging to the castle; he armed one end of it with a ram's horn, that it might be better fitted for defence; as soon as he delivered it to me, I began my Journey and left a place which I then feared I should never see again.

IL
[Hugh Brackenridge]

Chapter 3*d*

Ibam sacra forte via nescio quid Meditans.

Hor. Sat's

Thus, brethren, I left the castle, inly grieving at the immense Journey I was fated to perform in this wretched manner; my resolutions however surmounted all difficulties, tho' they bore exceeding hard upon me, for my huge Jack-boots pinched my toes prodigiously after I had travelled about a mile down the Lane which leads to the potter's field, so that I hobbled along instead of walking; nevertheless I persisted in my course, reading now and then in my book of the labours and travels of Peter the Hermit, for I had almost forgot to tell you that I carried several books in my wallet, which were if I remember right, Bunyan's Hymns, Peter the Hermit, an Alcoran and two volumes of Bailey's dictionaries which I intended as a present to Mahomet when I should arrive at Mecca. I very patiently stumbled along on foot with these, considering in the mean time what course I should take to reach the nearest sea-port town on this side of our Continent. After much thought I laid it out thus; first to travel on foot to New York, situated on an island of the same name, from thence to the palace of my father situated on the eastern shore of Long-island, where I proposed to refresh and prepare myself for a long and dangerous Voyage to the coast of Barbary in a Ship under the command of Commodore Russel,* and from thence to travel on foot over the burning sands of Africa 'till I should reach the city of Mecca in Arabia. Thus being fully resolved and having settled everything on this head, I jogged on in the most extreme tortures caused by my boots, 'till I reached the suburbs of Kingston; after I had entered the city I went into the shop of one Mustapha Alamanri who rendered my boots

* He was one of the Tory club and had a pair of kneebands 6 inches broad.

more pliable and comfortable to my feet; I then issued out of the stall and stepped into a Caravansera where I demanded a dram of the best West-India rum, two quarts of Cyder, a pint of Metheglin and 5 gills of Brandy; these I mixed together in a large bowl and clapping it to my head drank the whole composition off in less than two minutes; then I took a turn into the Kitchen and saw a mulatto boy turning a spit which contained a leg of mutton and half a dozen fowls pretty well roasted and almost ready to be served upon the Table. Hey, my friend, quoth I, who do these partridges belong to? Not to you, replied he. Ay faith, said I, say you so; I'll soon try that with you. Then directing the horned end of my staff to the spitt, I swept off three of the fowls and clapping them in my wallet made off thro' the back yard into another street, having first thrown the boy into a Tub of Hog's swill to prevent his alarming the house and thereby discovering me. By this time I felt pretty chearful and having got into another street, I hauled out one of my fowls and devoured it before a train of people who followed me out of curiosity to see the strange figure I made; they greatly revered me nevertheless on account of my long beard, nodding Turban and flowing vest which waved in the wind very gracefully, tho' the unreasonable width of the sleeves incommoded me somewhat as I soon after fatally experienced; for as I traversed the streets, reeling like a Drunkard (the liquor which I drank beginning to affect me very sensibly), a gentleman perceiving me from his window and knowing me to be a pilgrim by my habit instantly sent a little girl to invite me to dine with him. It being now pretty near noon, and my wallet not overloaded with provisions, I thankfully accepted his offer, but as I mounted the piazza to meet the Gentleman in his parlour, I had the misfortune to miss a step and being pretty top heavy I fell back into the street which shelving pretty much I rolled about half a dozen yards 'till I was stopped by a deep gutter in the middle of the street into which I was plunged; here I lay sometime belching up the rum and raw fowls into the dirty water, 'till the Gentleman perceiving my danger rushed out with a long rope and slipping it about my neck drew me out of that sink of corruption, where but for him I had breathed my last. As soon as I perceived myself on the ground I leaped up and, covered with Mud, ran into the house with great agility, where meeting the maid whom I mistook for the mistress, I accosted her thus, the liquor dropping all the time from my mouth: Pray-pray-pray, Mad-mad-madam how do you do-do-do, I have had the misfortune to fall into your de-de-devilish ditch before your door. Ay, quoth she, and I wish you had lain there till I helped you out, you impudent Jackanapes; what the plague does my master mean to be inviting every dirty vagabond in, that straggles along the road? Get this moment out of the parlour into the yard or, by heavens, I'll drive you out into the street faster than you came in. Ay, said I, is it the custom of your town to use pilgrims thus? Were you not one of that dastardly female crew whom my soul despises, you should this moment feel the weight of my invincible arm. Scarce had I spoke, when four country ruffians entered, and at the maid's persuasion, seized me by the collar and dragged me into the yard, where they soused me headlong into a pond of water, which they called a Bath, under pretence of cleansing me; at my first dive I was drove to the bottom with such fury, that my head stuck a considerable time in a ton of mud, my Turban floated on the surface and as to my boots they shared the same fate with myself; during the time I was on the bottom, I was thoroughly purified, so that when I came up I looked as fair and as handsome as ever; the fellows seeing the change in my appearance, took me on shore and having combed my head, and adjusted my Turban, they led me into the great parlour where was a most elegant feast provided. Ah, said the gentleman, I perceive you are come to your self again my good friend. Faith, answered I, I cannot say it, but I believe my vest, Turban, boots and other accoutrements have come to themselves, for I have had one of the most devilish sousings that ever was performed on any human creature, since the days of Noah, for immediately after you delivered me out of that filthy place in the street, four ugly Devils clasped me in their arms and plunged me into a large river where I have been swimming about these two hours. Ay, ay, said he, in that case then come don't be dejected, you have reason to rejoice, for I am sure you was in a woful pickle before. At these words I took courage and by the gentleman's invitation I sat down with him to dinner but did not finish it by reason of a cursed piece of ill fortune which soon after befell me: For when I was almost half satisfied, and was at an unhappy moment endeavouring to swallow the Gizzard of a Turkey, which being unable to digest I gave a violent belch, followed by above a quart of that mixed liquor and all I had eaten at this feast, which came full drive upon a dish of potatoes, which stood in the middle of the Table; this confused me so much, that, as I was bending my arms over the table to ask pardon, I swept off above half a dozen dishes of sauce with those monstrous sleeves I have so often complained of. This provoked the Gentleman so much that, unable to contain his rage, he started up and with a furious tone spoke thus: Ill-fated wretch who art travelling to thy own destruction, this moment depart from my door or by that devilish Turban, and those scandalous boots and detestable sleeves which have this day put my table into disorder, I will spurn thee headlong from that chair into the street. I was not much pleased with the latter part of his speech, but as I dared not reply, I got up and departed, more afflicted at losing my dinner than his friendship. From hence I resolved to pass by the eastern gate of the city and pursue my journey thro' the land of Raritan, but whilst I was putting this design in execution I met with a very rude fellow, who greatly ridiculed my Turban and holy garb, together with my boots and beard, and to such a degree did his impudence rise that he caught me by the whiskers and would surely have hauld me to the ground, had I not fetched him an hearty whack over the pate with the butt end of my staff and would instantly have killed him had not his brother Muley Melech strongly interceeded for his life, upon whose account I freely granted it, first making the rash youth swear upon the Alcoran that he never would insult a pilgrim again. I now reflected of what great use an Iron spike would be, in all future engagements, in one end of my cane, the ram's horn being on the other; this I resolved to have done before I left the city; therefore I entered the forge of one Solyman Houli Hhan and signifying my intention to him he immediately hammered out one about 8 inches long, fixed it neatly in the thick end of my staff, and bound it firmly with an Iron ring; then bidding him adieu I swung my dictionaries over my shoulder, seized my staff and in great haste issued out of the gate. In about four hours I had a view of the famous city Brunswick, which if I mistake not lies upon a certain branch of Raritan river. I travelled with all speed that I might reach it before sunset, which with some difficulty I effected. As I entered the city I asked several persons if there were any houses of public entertainment for Pilgrims; I was answered, there were several Taverns for gentlemen but none for such a wretched miscreant as I appeared to be. Woe to me and my father's house, thought I, with myself, shall I be obliged to lie in the street then! No, by my boots, I'll assert the dignity of Pilgrims in this distant land, let the consequence be what it will; so resolved, I marched courageously up to the first house I saw have a sign posted at it, and fetching a violent rapp on the door demanded admittance. Who's there? said somebody within; Somebody worse than the Devil himself unless you instantly let him in. As soon as they heard this immediately the Maid double locked the door, ran up stairs and discharged a flood of urine upon my head pot and all; this terrible accident disordered my Turban a little but I remained perfectly calm and quiet in my mind and not seeming to take any notice of it, gave the door another violent blow and once more demanded entrance; otherwise, continued I, I shall scale your walls and put you all to the

death of the ram's horn and iron spike. Terrified at these menaces they at last admitted me. Ye scum of the earth! Ye base
born monsters, said I, is this the usage you give to Pilgrims, who
are obliged to endure all kinds of hardships, while you live in
ease and plenty? They excused themselves as well as they could
and declared, if they had known I was a pilgrim, I should have
been admitted at the first word. Well, well, said I, I pardon you
this offence but never let me hear the like of you again, for when
I am enraged my vengeance knows no bound; but pray, continued I, let me have something for supper, for the devil a
mouthful have I eat since I left Kingston. Yes, yes, quoth the
landlady, your honour shall have something in an instant; she
was as good as her word, and when I had supped to my heart's
content, I desired them to show me to bed, seeing I was exceedingly wearied with my Journey; this they also complied with and
conducted me into a very old and gloomy Garret, in which stood
three beds or rather traps, for such they appeared to me, hardly
able to support the bed-clothes on them tho' they were not over-
plenty, but rather the contrary; such was the appearance of my
bedchamber, with which being pretty much vexed, I expostulated
thus with the maid who held the candle for me. Pray, Madam, is
this the best entertainment you have in the house for a person of
my dignity? Sir, said she, we have other beds, but we keep them
for gentlemen. Gentlemen! quoth I, and pray what the devil do
you imagine I am; this moment vanish from my presence, or, by
my beard, I'll send you headlong downstairs, as if the devil himself was after you. She immediately dropped the candle and fled,
which I picked up before it went out and set it in its proper place;
then loosing my wallet, I pulled out the first volume of Bailey's
Dictionaries and had not read half a dozen pages, when there
entered several clownish fellows, who, it seems, were yeomen
and waggon-drivers; they took not the least notice of me, but
threw themselves into the other beds and in a few moments fell a
snoring like Hogs. After I had read half an hour longer I closed

the book and prepared for bed, but taking a nearer view of the structure and furniture of it, I could not help wondering at its peculiarity; Bless me, said I, nothing but two boards and a blanket that a dog would not lie on, prepared for a person of my dignity; Well, well, Pilgrims can't always expect easy lodgings, but in the morning I'll let them know I expected it in such a place as this. When I had said this I blew out my lamp and in the height of my anger threw myself very forcibly upon my hard couch, but o terrible how was I surprized, when I found myself driven with the swiftness of a cannon bullet thro' the garret, losing one half my right ear in my flight, and soused head foremost among the clownish waggoners I mentioned. Hey, said one of them who was awake, who have we here? That cursed Wizzard, answered another, whom we saw reading when we came to bed. Alas my friends, said I, I am no wizzard, only a pilgrim travelling a journey upon a religious account; By my life, replyed the fellow, can't you travel your journies without disturbing honest people who want nothing but their night's sleep? No you are a witch, I swear by my waggon and horses, and you shall instantly suffer for it; so saying, they endeavoured to tye me up in a blanket designing to pound me to death, but by the favour of the holy prophet, I engaged them all with my bare fists, and in less than a quarter of an hour, put them to flight. Some ran down stairs and broke into the street, others clambered down the wall, so that I had the whole garret in my possession 'till morning, at which time I examined into the cause of the elasticity of my bed and found that it was caused by an artificial contrivance in order to perplex and hurt unwary strangers. As I had not much liking to this chamber I hunted about for the half part of the ear I had lost, and had the good fortune to find it hanging upon a rusty nail. I secured it in my wallet and hastened down stairs resolving to destroy the whole Family for their insolence; but upon second thoughts contented myself with giving them a sound drubbing from the Eldest to the youngest; I also tore down the sign and sign-post and threw them into the river, depriving them at the same time of their Licence to keep Tavern 'till the tenth generation downwards. Thus having punished these monsters and well replenished my wallet I pursued my Journey towards the metropolis Amboy, with great peace of mind and inward quiet. But you shall have the particulars of this Journey in my next harangue.

JΓ
[Philip Freneau]

Chapter 4*th*

Romulum post hos _____
_____ memorem?

HOR. LIB. 10. 12

Having travelled some distance I saw a chimney top appear, pointing to the firmament, which I found to proceed from a Caravansera on the way for the entertainment of strangers. Here I met with a learned Bramin, of the sect of Omar, by name Aliborah the skipper. The devout musselman soon struck up a friendship with me and gave me the history of his life in the following words:

The History of Aliborah the Skipper.

I dwell in the mighty castle built by Mahomet III^d and which now belongs to the sultan of the Indies and lies about 3 miles west of the great city of Kingston. In this castle are many spacious Apartments, furnished with carpets, sofas and Maps for the use and amusement of the religious Bramins who have dwelt there time immemorial. My apartment lyeth near the top of the Building on the south side of an oblong square, called the upper entry; from my windows I have a beautiful and extensive prospect of the country all round. In this happy and pleasing solitude I lived for many years, perusing the writings of the faithful and spending the hours so unwisely squandered away by others in the devout exercises of a true Musselman or composing sonnets and madrigals with all the flowing tropes of the oriental Magi. In the lower entry of this castle was a mosque of Dervises, who were unfortunately bewitched by a deceitful Gypsey, suborned by the Mamaluke of Egypt, whose name was Endella, Sardi Jaff, skilled in the powers of Necromancy and the spells of the inferior Genii. The Dervises were suddenly taken with an enthusiastic fit of

Poetry and imagined themselves of the first magnitude. One of them wrote the history of Nimrod and according to the sentiments of the Judicious the piece reflected great dishonour upon the author. A poem was likewise published by subscription, entitled, "The poet's confession," wherein he was introduced giving an account of numerous sins by him committed. But it was known for a truth that he never had been guilty of the crimes which he confessed, but that it was dictated to him by some evil spirit which made use of his poetical Organ to disgrace the practice of the faithful. In the mean time an aged Gentleman of the sect of Ali named Giran al Canto, who had been himself tormented with the false spirit, but recovered, spoke on this occasion with calmness and in a very diverting manner. But to the purpose: the disturbances continued in the mosque and I was obliged at last to undertake to pacify them; accordingly I composed a piece wrote in the true eastern stile and surnamed it The Skipper's.* This poem was carried on in a kind of ruthless rhyme and nobly done, but as I had unfortunately wrote it in imitation of the Delphic Oracles and filled it with the dark and mysterious sayings of the Bramins it was unintelligible to natural men. I applied to an ancient Dervise versed in the Runic rhymes who translated and corrected my performance; I exulted in the great glory of producing something to the advantage of the age and my memory. But how was I deceived; the dear offspring of my brain, my first born, was trampled under foot and I underwent an universal

---

* A wretched poem wrote in defence of Bombo's natomen, a strange term made use of in this poem. But as some may be desirous of knowing what sort of a thing the Skipper was, I shall here subjoin the beginning of it:

> The duellists are to blame I fear
> But why should long the cloke of shame to wear;
> If in it was always under prudence kept
> Whoever rallied would be circumspect;
> Beware, beware ye presumptuous youth
> For who, I humbly beg, are you forsooth?

hiss as I returned to my chamber, reflecting on the vicious taste of mankind.

Here the Bramin ended his story and I prepared to prosecute my Journey, but he informed me he would travel on foot with me as far as the city of Amboy, from whence, continued he, I intend to go to New York in a boat and then I'll put myself on board Commodore Russel's ship, who is preparing for a voyage to the coast of Barbary, whither I will accompany him as a domestic companion. Most reverend Aliborah, said I, how fortunately have we met at this caravansera; I myself am travelling toward the same port as yourself and intend to embarque in the same vessel, bound to the same place with you upon my way to Mecca. Ay, then, replied he, we shall be companions a long time. I hope so, returned I; we can travel together to the port of Amboy, from whence you say you are to depart in a sloop; for my part the laws and customs of Pilgrims oblige me to go on foot every inch of the Journey, except where an unavoidable necessity compels me to do otherwise. After I had said this we packed up and directed our faces towards Amboy. But my Turban being rather too high, as I went along was at last entangled in the thick branches of an oak that overhung the way and had not the Prophet sent me a Janizary riding upon a Mule, I should certainly have been hanged, but was disengaged by his favour, whose name was Belridan Alrad. We then passed on conversing on the unstable nature of all human enjoyments and the many disasters to which Pilgrims are exposed.

IL
[Hugh Brackenridge]

Chapter 5th

Nemo me impune lacessit.

QUEEN MARY'S MOTTO.

In a few hours we arrived at the metropolis Amboy where Aliborah immediately embarqued for New York. As it was now past sunset, I looked about me for a lodging, but by reason of my strange appearance could not prevail upon any person to take me in and I durst not proceed to violence least I should have been torn to pieces by the vulgar who followed me gaping as much as if I had been Mahomet himself; finding myself therefore put to this pinch, and my belly growing very unruly, I hastened down to the river side and picked up a number of large oysters which I opened and devoured with great content and serenity of mind; after I had satisfied myself, I concluded to continue my Journey by moon-light to the town of Elizabeth, which I doubted not but I could reach by next morning at farthest, and indeed I was far from being mistaken for by the time the sun rose it began to appear at a distance; the lofty spires, balconies and battlements and the roofs of the Edifeces covered with cedar, afforded a most delightful prospect. Elizabeth is situated on a beautiful river and is at this day inhabited by christians. As I approached nearer, I could perceive the buildings were all compleated in the five orders of architecture, in the study of which I have spent a good deal of my time and I must do myself the honour to say that it was I who plotted, planned and projected the famous building the castle in which I spent the first part of my life.

It was early on Christmass morning when I entered the Town, and notwithstanding the excessive severity of the weather, there were upwards of an hundred students skating on the Ice on the river and playing in the great square of the Town. Having been bred a gentleman I was resolved to shew them the fruits of a finished education, and that I was not an unpolished rustic, devoid of learning and good manners; I accordingly accosted them in a very courteous manner, with an elegant latin introduction, salve Domine, but just at this time recollecting that I was run short of money, I betook myself to one of my ingenious tricks in order to replenish my pouch with a few shillings to provide the viaticum or provisions for travelling; I pulled out my Xenophon and offered to sell it to the young gentlemen, for I supposed them to be scholars. In the twinkling of a cow's thumb, for I love to tell a straight story, above an hundred of them came gaping around me expressing great surprize at my unusual garb and I must confess, my dress was somewhat strange, as it does not become a Pilgrim to deck himself with the vain superfluities of the man of the world. Young Gentlemen, said I, pulling out my book, this is a valuable author and the best edition of him, as I have corrected him with my own hand, by expunging the particle καὶ* which destroys the harmony of the words; it is likewise my intention, said I, to favour the world with a new print of the works of the ancient humorist Lucian, by extracting the particle οὐκ, which spoils the beauty of the verse, to render him more agreeable to this refined age. As I was talking in this manner they gave me an instance of the impudence and audacious boldness of depraved nature by raising a general laugh to my great surprize and astonishment; hereupon I began to reprove them in a sober and judicious manner on the impropriety of their behaviour, but the evil Genii, the enemies of the faithful, blindfolded their eyes, and stopped their ears to my salutary instructions; these insults produced a downright quarrel; one of the malicious crew took me by the collar and endeavoured to supplant me by a trip; provoked at the Usage, I smote him upon the head with my staff, and fixing the horned end under his chin I

* Bombo, when he was a student in the University, took upon him to censure Xenophon for the redundancy of the particle καὶ and accordingly struck it out with a rusty horse-nail wherever he met with it. And as this was approved by the dean and principal, he took upon him to make the same refinement in Lucian with respect to the particle οὐκ.

twirled him around in the air, but as I was thus playing Hercules upon him, another of the band mounting on the shoulders of his accomplices, took hold of my Turban and swung by it like a witch in a steeple till he brought me backwards full drive in the street; in the meantime another laying hold of my wallet, began to thresh me with the books as a scotchman does pease, then a dozen more of them catching me by the legs, drew me a furlong down the street. To my inexpressible sorrow I lost my staff and Turban in the scuffle; enraged then like a wild boar I made sudden and strenuous effort; leaping to my feet I pulled off one of my boots, and began to lay about me so that I brought them down like ripe Pissimmons. I hope I may say without being suspected of exaggerating the matter beyond the bounds of strict truth that I there performed immortal actions, slaying seven at a blow, discomfiting three men armed with scythes, and sundering the head of a Miller from his body who came against me with a pick-ax in one hand and a crowbar in the other. Now gathering a fresh supply of strength, by exercising, as a snowball by rolling, I broke the necks of two oxen that roared against me, trod down three horsemen with whom I encountered, leaped into a yard and slew a Doctor and his son; sallying thence I made my way thro' a file of soldiers that stood in my way. Now my imagination was on the wing, I began to figure to myself everlasting wreaths of fame as the reward of my uncontrouled courage; but here fortune, the mistress of the world, the enemy of the brave and valiant, unluckily for me stepped in, and changed the current of the day. I was resolved to defy her, but to show her prowess, she brought against me a mighty giant whose name was Mohrou Bedowin the son of the hills, a hunter of racoons and a great warrior among men; he is a mighty scholar of Pythagoras, he remembered the time when he lived in the land of Nod and founded the Assyrian monarchy; his mental part, for that never changes, was conveyed down thro' various shapes and forms, sometimes he animated the body of a cock, sometimes a horse and more frequently an ass.

This Giant as soon as he beheld my heroic appearance and

various warlike accoutrements, dyed and stained with the blood of the vanquished, appeared in a maze of perplexity and confusion, but spurred on by the fury of his own distraction, he threw his Javelin at me, full three cloth yards in length, but by a dexterity peculiar to myself I avoided it; hereupon I made a pass at him, but unfortunately shivered a spear, which I had picked up in the fray, into a thousand pieces, on his burnished armour, which was proof against metal. Encouraged by this accident he came on like the rushing wind of the North, and taking me by the beard swung me as high as the steeple, but by the power of Gravitation and the weight of my Body I came down sorely bruised by a fall which would have disordered a frame composed of any common materials; taking me then by the nape of the neck, he turned me round, as a butcher does the head of a calf when he tries its weight; I should certainly have died by his hands, had I not bethought myself of a very humorous and necessary expedient: Like the fox in the fable I caught him by the Testicles and thus bring down his huge carcase, as a mountain oak beside a stream; then putting my heel in his neck I trod out his breath, and to be humorous upon him I desired he would send me an account of his voyage over the river Styx in Charon's boat. Now thanking fortune for her kind condescension I intreated her to extend it something farther, which I had no sooner done but her majesty who is wont to shift like a weather-cock pointed out my staff and Turban lying about a pole distant from where I then was; having likewise extorted a confession from one of the prisoners, I found my wallet in a cellar where he had hid it. Resolving to stay no longer in so unhospitable a place, I marched off taking the high road leading to the ferry at the mouth of Hudson's river, designing to embark from thence for long-island and thence to travel by land to my father's palace situated three day's Journey from the spacious Haven of Nova-Yanka.

IL
[Hugh Brackenridge]

Chapter 6th

_____ Cæsarem vehis

ANON

The man for wisdom's various arts renown'd
Long exercis'd in woes; O Muse resound
Who when his aims had wrought the destin'd fall
Of many a chief _____
Wand'ring from shore to shore obedient stray'd
The people noted and their realms survey'd.

HOMER'S ODYSSEY

I soon arrived at the ferry, where, by good luck, I saw an Oyster boat putting from the shore; I immediately ran down in great speed to prevent their leaving me, and hailed them thro' one of my boots instead of a speaking trumpet; Ho! the ship Ho! will you take a pilgrim aboard! ho! The fellows in the boat seeing me (for as they afterwards told me they heard not a word I said, as my voice was confined in my boot) immediately tacked about and came ashore and by that time I was got to the water side too; Hey! said I, take me aboard this moment and carry me to the other side. And pray what will you give us for our trouble? said one of them. What will I give you? answered I, I'll give you the honour, that's enough. The Honour! quoth the other, great honour to be sure, to be had from a scarecrow flying away in rags; wait here, continued he, my friend, 'till you can find persons generous or foolish enough to accept your offer; so saying, they were upon the point of leaving me, when finding that threats would do no good, I proceeded to intreaties and begged them by my sacred personage to waft me over. They then whispered to each other, something I could not hear; at last the youngest of the two spoke to me thus: We consent to carry you over without any freight-money, provided you stand up in the midst of the boat instead of a sail, for as we are tired of rowing, you and your ragged garments will drive us over in a hurry before this favourable gale. Tho I perceived they did all this for their diversion, yet to get over at any rate, I consented to the proposal and was instantly haled on board and placed standing in the midst with my face towards the prow; as the waves ran pretty high, it was agreed I could not stand steady unless I was secured by stays and shrowds. This I also consented to as reasonable. Then to my unspeakable pain they tied cords round my ears and fastened them to the sides of the vessel. Thus I stood, Mast, sail and all, when they loosed the skiff from shore. The wind blew most vehemently and the steersman kept our vessel full before the gale; my Turban bowed before the blast, and my holy garb which was sadly torn waved about like a set of streamers; to make short of the matter we plowed the deep with an amazing velocity, and in a little space reached the western shore of long-Island. They thinking I had paid sufficiently for my ferrying unbound me and left me to my own free will. I then swung my wallet over my shoulder and ascended an high bank, where I had a delightful view of the sea and adjacent country; descending from hence, I kept along the road and at length came to a large pile of buildings which I found was the seat of a country-gentleman, who had lately retired from the hurry of business to enjoy a rural repose. Surely, said I to myself, I shall find people more hospitable in this my native Island than in the places thro' which I passed; however to know the real thoughts of the inhabitants of this house concerning me, I will feign myself deaf and they not suspecting the veracity of my word, will say what they please before me. Full of this scheme I entered the yard and saw an elderly man sitting on the piazza; pray Sir, said I, if you have any thing to say, hollow very loud, as I am almost stone deaf, or make signs with your hand. He accordingly chose the latter of these proposals and by his motions desired me to sit with him; I accepted the favour, and striding across the courtyard with my huge boots deposited my breech on the same bench with him. And pray Sir, said I, what book is this (for he was reading). As he thought I could not hear he showed me the title page. But, bless me, how was I astonished to see that it contained an account of the first part of my own adventures! The sight of it made me blush at first and I laughed heartily at several of them; I resolved however not to discover my self, lest the gentleman should be too kind seeing my name was transmitted to posterity before I was half dead. Well Sir, said I, this is an odd kind of an history, the adventures are almost innumerable and the incidents surprizing! pray sir, do you know who is the author of it? This man, said he, keeps asking me questions perpetually and expects I should answer him altho' he told me an hour ago he was as deaf as a stone or a log. Hand my speaking trumpet down, said he to a wench, that I may tell him who are the Authors of this history; this she instantly did and he clapping it to my Ears roared out these words: The common report is that this history is wrote by two Bramins residing in the castle of Nassau. Ay, ay, said I, almost stunned with the sound, I understand you perfectly well. Then to divert his wife and family, he read the 2ᵈ. and 3ᵈ. Chapters concerning Nadir Gaw's singeing my beard, and the sweeping of the victuals off the table at Kingston &ca. Well faith, said I, the history runs very smooth, the stile is rapid, and the language genuine and polite. How know you that, quoth he, I read with a very low voice and you told me a while ago you could not hear one word spoken low? Sir, replied I, your honour does me great wrong to suppose that I am deceiving you. No, I swear by Mahomet, I can't hear more than a block. And pray when did you loose your hearing, said he? I lost it, replied I, about sixteen weeks ago, by a great cold occasioned by falling into an horse pond. Well, upon my word, said he, it is a sad thing to lose one's hearing, but I perceive you have lost one half your right ear, how happened that? Have you left it on the whipping post or is it nailed on the Jail door? Alas, Mahomet forbid, said I, that ever I should arrive at that honour; No Sir, I lost it by accident, but luckily found it again and at present have it secured in my saddle bags. Your saddle bags, quoth he, what do you ride an horse then? Od's my life, answered I, I can't hear a word you say; by my troth, I can only see the moving of your lips. You lying Rascal, said he, have you not been answering all the questions I have put to you this half hour, and now when you have recollected and find yourself detected, you deny a thing that you have ignorantly confessed yourself. I found myself unable to form an answer to what he said, much more to deny what was so plain and all the recource that was now left me was to ask the pardon of the whole family, and the master of the house in particular, for the confounded trick I had almost played them. But this availed me nothing; he was so terribly enraged that he peremptorily commanded me to depart his house and not stay a minute longer; I was glad to come off so safely and immediately obeyed, taking the kitchen in my way under pretence of lighting my pipe, but in reality to filch a Gammon of bacon, which I easily effected; I accordingly clapped it into my wallet and pursued my Journey, altho' the sun was now set. I wished then, I had acquainted him, I was the very Bombo the history mentioned; I am sure he would have pardoned my fault and entertained me some days. Full of such reflections I travelled along with my wallet and Gammon, 'till I perceived by my Eyes it was pretty late and as I saw no houses (for the moon shone bright) I determined to take up my quarters on a large woody mountain, I saw at a distance on the left side of the road, but before I went thither I saw a chrystal stream, in which (like a good musselman) having washed my hands and quenched my thirst, I ascended the top of the mountain, where I found a convenient place for sleeping on a dry parcel of leaves, under a thick tuft of grape vines and Oaks which formed a natural bower. Before I closed my eyes, I resolved to take a luncheon of my Gammon which I doubted not would taste excellent to a stomach circumstanced as mine was; with this resolution I struck up a large fire with my knife and flint, beside a rock adjoining the place of my repose. This served to dress my food and defend me from the inclemency of the weather and the fury of wild beasts whom I could hear howling all thro' the woods and whose horrible yells would certainly have put me into some consternation had I not been a person of undoubted intrepidity. After I finished my repast on the Gammon, I renewed my fire and laid myself down to take a sound nap. But before I had slept two hours I was awaked by a strange apparition which terrified me exceedingly in spite of my valour. The moon was down and I could perceive by the Pleiades it was 12 o'Clock or midnight, when I could plainly see between me and the remains of the fire which were yet burning, an ugly kind of a creature somewhat white; its Eyes gave a most dismal glare and looked at me with all the fury imaginable; sometimes it advanced towards me, at other times retreated farther back, still keeping its eyes fixed on mine and threatening destruction every moment. Woe is me! cryed I, this is the Devil come to demand the Bacon I have stolen; I then searched my wallet to see if he had not taken it while I slept, but I found it safe under my head as I had placed it before. The apparition still kept its former situation between me and the fire tho' advancing a little nearer every minute. At last roused by fear, I accosted him thus. Pray, Mr. Satan, who are you, I wonder, that had the impudence to disturb my nightly slumbers in this solitary place? Has the smell of my Bacon, which I have been roasting, brought you here? Or have you any design upon my person? Neither; be assured I am resolved to defend both with all my might. This Bacon is my second self, my chief support 'till I reach the palace of my father, and I hope you will have more regard to your own safety than to attempt taking it away either by fair means or foul. So saying I armed myself with my Boots, for the Phantom did not seem terrified at my menaces; and snatching up my staff, I advanced boldly up and gave him a stroke, with the horned end of my staff, over the rump. This enraged him so that turning his posteriors he discharged above a Gallon of the most unsavoury urine that ever saluted my nostrils, directly into my face and eyes; the smart gave me intolerable pain; nevertheless, cryed I, By Mahomet, I'll try whose weapon will have most effect; I then made a pass at him with my spike, which I drove thro' his body, and hung him upon a tree till the morning. The Urine, that I received, pealed the skin off my face and I verily believe would have deprived me of my eyes had I not rushed down to the aforementioned brook and cleansed them and my cloaths, yet not so well, but that the offensive scent continued with me several days and I verily believe I have imbibed some tincture of it in my skin 'till this very moment. However I slumbered very quietly the remainder of the night and next day found my terrible Apparition to be no more than what the Dutch call a Stinkbingsen and the Turks a skunk. I was vehemently enraged to think I should be so frighted by such a silly animal and resolved that my fury end with his life; accordingly I erected a gibbet and strung him up, after singeing off his beard and tail, leaving him in this posture to bleach in the sun and rain; I then directed my course to the great road which I reached in a quarter of an hour; here I travelled four days without any remarkable adventure except destroying a wild bull which infested the country. The fifth day I saw my father's palace, hoping here to spend a week or two of a civilized life with pleasure, since I had met with nothing but blows and drubbings since I left the castle. However in this I was mistaken as by the sequel will appear. My father was chief commander in the palace and consequently pretty rich so that tho' his family were numerous, they were well provided for in all the necessaries of life, so that when I came near the house the Dogs who had not seen for a long time such a ragged person as myself, rushed out upon me and would have tore me to pieces had not a sturdy servant delivered me; thus I had been almost torn to pieces at my own threshold after surmounting so many other dangers. But my father hearing such a terrible uproar among the dogs, for I almost lamed some of them with the horned end of my staff, ran out with a long horse-whip and before he knew what he was about gave me a severe trimming as supposing I had set the Dogs 'a fighting. What the Devil! roared I, is not enough to be trounced all the way since I left the castle but here at home must I be flogged like a Dog with a horsewhip for nothing? And pray who are you, said he, that call this your home? Beans and Pumpkins, said I, don't you know your own son Bombo? Have you not the history of my life in your house? I have read it fifty times in different places since I left the castle. Ay, ay, said he, are you Bombo then? No, I have not seen your history nor heard of it. But pray what brings you home strolling on foot in this beggarly manner? You look like Beelzebub himself flying away in rags. By my hand, were it not a long time since I saw you last, I would order you instantly to be hung up in my cornfields in quality of a scarecrow; but come in, said he, and tell me the reason of your leaving the castle and be assured if you don't give a satisfactory answer to whatever questions I shall propose, I will send you back faster than you came. I accordingly entered, and told him the whole cause as related in the beginning of this Book; he then was satisfied and told me he would permit me to persevere in my Journey seeing it was by the command of the prophet. I then stepped into the great hall with an intention to salute my Brothers and Sisters, but they instantly fled at my approach, as thinking it had been the Devil coming for them. I returned immediately to my father and desired him to furnish me with a suit of cloaths to wear while at home and also to provide me a new Turban, vest, and boots against I should depart; this he consented to and I was supplied with present necessaries out of the wardrobe, tho' my boots I retained, and strutted about very majestically. It seems I was grown very rustic in my travels by conversing with so many uncivilized nations, for which my father often rebuked me and promised at my departure to give me a sett of instructions for my more polite behaviour. Then I passed the remainder of the day in jollity, conversing very sociably with the family who now recollected my features and knew me again; some of the children, however, were very shy on account of my beard which was now near fourteen inches in length.

At night it was my lot to sleep with a weaver that belonged to the palace. As I sat up pretty late discoursing about my travels, when I came to bed I found him snoring like a hog; and as I had been used so long to sleep on boards and in the woods, without undressing myself, I jumped in by his side boots, breeches and all. Long had I not slept when I heard him growl most grievously, which I found proceeded from some violent kicks I had given him in my sleep with my boots; he at last waked in a violent passion and finding me lying with my boots on, and feeling his shanks battered at a terrible rate, concluded, in a minute, that I was the cause of it, and in retaliation gave me a most violent blow on the face with his fist so that my countenance was nothing but a gore of blood; not content with this, he rose and taking me by the boots, dragged me out of bed and thro' the room; after he had sufficiently wearied himself with this sport afforded at my expence, he crowded me under the bed. I was determined if possible not to be in such a mean place, and kicked and roared most terribly in order to disengage myself; my father hearing such a noise came to enquire into the cause of it; he entered and by the light of a lamp which he brought with him saw the weaver pushing me under the bed and accosted him thus in a rage: Gregory (for that was the weaver's name) why don't you let that cursed bawler alone, who has come home on purpose to plague and vex me? Let him alone! quoth he, rather why does he not let me alone? Look at my shins, Sir, and then ask me why I don't let him alone. Come out, Bombo, said my father, and answer for the rudeness you have committed on Gregory's shins. I did not chuse to obey this lest I should receive a second drubbing and therefore lay as still as a mouse, pretending to be fast asleep, but this stratagem did not succeed; for my father ordering the Weaver to lay hold of my boots and drag me into the middle of the floor, he obeyed with great alacrity and in the twinkling of a dead Bear's Eye; my father gave me fifty or sixty of the severest Bastinadoes ever human creature got; this forced me to open my eyes and pretending to be just awake I cryed out, O terrible! terrible, what a dream I have had; I just fancied I was beating a monstrous Giant to death with my boots, as he endeavoured to steal my wallet and Turban! Aye, says Gregory, and your dream was but too true in part, for you have almost battered my shins to pieces with your confounded Boots, tho' heaven forbid I should steal your wallet which I verily believe with all its contents is not worth a farthing; when the matter was a little cleared up, my father committed me to Gregory's care the remainder of the night, who insisted I should disengage myself from the boots before I entered the bed again; it was in vain that I insisted on the privileges due to Pilgrims; he would by no means consent, 'till at last the debate was finished by granting one boot to Gregory and retaining the other myself, to be on an equal footing if any disturbance should arise thro' the remainder of the night. Thus we slept 'till morning when the weaver returned me my boot and went to his loom; and I went to read in my dictionaries of which I had finished the 1st Volume and made surprizing progress in the 2^{d} and indeed I must own Bailey is an excellent author for which reason I often noted down several of his observations in my common-place book that I might have them ready for use on every occasion and it was not long 'till I had an opportunity of showing my knowledge; for my father asking me one day what was the Summum Bonum, or chief good of mankind? faith, Sir, answered I, it is a pretty hard question but if I may be allowed to speak my sentiments of the matter, I would say that flogging and trouncing a person, as I have been ever since I left the castle besides not less than two hundred Bastinadoes which I have had from your Worship since I had the honour to come home, I say this does him more good than any thing else, as for Instance Bayley saith in the 2189th Page Vol. 1st: "Of all discourses and writings none are so profitable or useful to mankind as those which have been often corrected and polished"; My father applauded the answer and commended me for the knowledge I had laid up. But not to detain you unnecessarily, I spent three weeks at home in this manner, at the end of which Time I put my father in mind of the Obligation I was under to visit New York as I was there to go aboard Commodore Russel's ship on my intended voyage. Hereupon he promised I should be dismissed early next morning. In the meantime I tryed on a new pair of Boots made of the dry hide of a brindle ox untanned, the hairy side was outward and the Horns stuck behind instead of spurs; their fashion also was somewhat different from the others as they served both for boots and breeches at once. A new Garb and Turban were also provided for me made out of coarse cloth and well tarred all over to guard against the casualties of wind and rain. In the evening, my father gave me a paper of instructions concerning my future behaviour but as these were pretty tedious I shall pass them over and just say that each of them was worth its weight in Gold. Next morning by break of day I was properly accoutred for my journey and kissed my Mother and sisters and bade farewell to my father and Brothers; I wept heartily, tho' they did not mind it a straw and to tell the truth I believe they were heartily tired of my company. However be this as it will I departed and at the end of three days reached the city of New York. But my adventures here I must reserve for the 1st Chapter of the next Book.

The End of the first Book.

JΓ
[Philip Freneau]

Father Bombo's
Pilgrimage to Mecca

Book the Second

Chapter 1st

_____ si propius stes _____
_____ te capiat magis.

HORACE

_____ the nearer you behold
_____ the more it strikes you.

━━━━━

———— *A true story* ————

Dear brethren!

By the time I had reached the suburbs of New York, grey
twilight had stretched her sable curtains o'er one half the globe,
the droning beetles wheeled their flight and the drousy tinklings
of the steeple bells inclined the minds of the serious to sober
thought. I had determined to lodge in the streets as a way-faring
man, like the Moabite of old when he came to a city of Gilead,
untill I considered the dangerous tendency of the night air and
the noxious vapours arising from the water, for, if I remember
right Aristotle has a precept somewhere to this purpose:

> Let every trav'ling Wight
> Avoid the damps of night
> Before the vapours have
> Sent him to his grave.

Accordingly I pushed up the main street to the sign of the twelve
pigeons, but seeing several persons walking in the Piazza, daubed
with gold and the like ensigns of Pride, I found it was a house
of entertainment for persons of quality and therefore to procure
a lodging there was a task too great for the slender contents of

my purse. Now standing and musing a while I took a chew of the betelnut and pushed thro' a back alley to the sign of the Lady's Glove. This emblem of chastity made such a deep impression on my mind that I resolved to take up my lodging here; the first person that met me was an elderly lady apparently about 50 years of age, dressed in a very odd manner for one of her years and discretion. Madam, said I, I have prevailed on myself to spend this night under your roof, 'till the morning returns to welcome me on my way to the holy-land, nor shall I stand on any ceremony with you, as I imagine a full purse is the best recommendation in this place. Sir, replied she, with an air that bespoke her good-breeding and civility, you are extremely welcome to my assistance for a lodging; please to walk into this chamber, and I will send the hostler to take care of your horse. A horse? Madam, said I, I assure you I have no such useless implements; I am a pilgrim walking on foot to the holy land. I ask pardon Sir, replied she, I was led into this mistake by seeing you booted and spurr'd contrary to the custom of footmen; however please to walk in and recline upon that sofa, while I go and send a young damsel to wait upon you, for as you appear to be a person in the bloom of his years and your hair of a reddish cast I fancy you cannot be insensible to the charms of the fair sex. The fair sex? Madam, answered I, by the charms of Venus, I am a professed admirer of the whole female world; hereupon I reclined upon the Sofa and waited with the greatest impatience 'till a young lady in the bloom of fifteen made her appearance; I immediately jumped up and saluted her with a kiss; I now was beginning to anticipate the joys between a sincere lover and his willing fair one but was interrupted by the voice of a person at the door who proved to be the landlady, telling me that there was a Gentleman just arrived and desired to know if I would suffer him to have a share of my room; determined to show my politeness on every Occasion, I sent word to the Gentleman to walk in; accordingly in a few minutes he entered the chamber and seated himself upon the Sofa where the young lady and I were reclining. After some time I observed his eyes scarcely keeping time with his tongue but now and then giving a side look on the fair one whom I encircled in my arms; filled with Jealousy, I rose in a great fury, called for my staff and resolved to repay him for his indecent intrusion; Sir, says he, I am no bully but if you will take a fair round in the room here I will never fail you. Upon this we began with the courage of Heroes in the day of battle; the shaking of the room was like an Earthquake. This with the screaming of the Lady soon brought the whole house about our ears; the old lady called in the hostler to part us; his endeavours together with the intreaties of the women prevailed with us to compose matters and not destroy ourselves when so many fair ladies in the land wanted husbands. Madam, said I, I am very well satisfied with the drubbing I have given this impertinent fellow whom you introduced, provided you immediately order him to withdraw. Things being thus adjusted, I shut the door and betook myself to the Arms of the Lady again, and in this manner I spent the Evening 'till suppertime; after I had supped in a noble and sumptuous apartment (for I was resolved to live one night at least like a Gentleman) I called for my bed, which after it was got ready I laid myself down in, having begged the lady to call upon me in about an hour's time; now considering it was not Gregory the weaver I was to have for a bed-fellow tonight I thought it expedient to pull off my boots. Then calling for the Jack I was answered there was none, but, said the Landlady, I will send in the hostler to help them off; he accordingly came and when I held up my leg he strode across it and laid out his whole strength in order to disengage them from my legs while I held fast by the bedpost, but the hide was so stiff and unpliant that with all his force he could not effect it; at last exerting all his might he made one sudden effort, but instead of drawing off the boot, tore down the bed and curtains upon me and strained my body as if it had been drawn in quarters

41

by wild horses, but the fellow himself, slipping his hold, ran head foremost out of the room and falling across an entry drove open a large door which opened into the Lady's dressing room. Now the house was in an uproar, for he had like to have discovered the nakedness of the family. In one corner of the room stood the old lady, who was just going to bed, shivering as if she had seen a Ghost; in another corner stood a damsel with her false paintings in her hand, for in these places the defects of age give way to the ingenuity of art. The young lady before mentioned broke forth like a fury to punish me for the wild uproar I had made; she flew at me with her nails and would certainly have done an injury to my eyes but that taking her by the ears, I jerked her forward with such violence that the whole forepart of her head came away. Woe is me! quoth I, I have committed murder; but I was soon relieved from my distress, by finding that what I took for half the skull was nothing else but a piece of parchment constructed in the form of a face, done off with false eye-brows, a fictitious nose and chin and paintings on the cheeks to deceive the simple and amorous stranger. The Hag who before I mistook for a young lady, being now divested of her false plaister stood motionless; how was I surprized to see her features shrivelled up like a Gourd, her eyes hollow and her chin bent up like the ram's horn on the end of my staff! How were all my amorous affections cooled when I beheld my inchanting fair one, converted into an old woman of seventy or eighty, a haggard, ugly, monstrous creature, more like the witch of Endor than any honest woman. The Landlady had by this time dressed herself and came running in a great rage. You vile dog, said she, you Rascal, you Jackanapes; did you come here to turn the house upside down and bring a bad report on the family? No, madam, answered I, I am a Gentleman, I was bred a Scholar, I meant you no harm; but as this accident has happened, let us smooth it up as well as we can; for there is nothing but ups and downs in this world, one misfortune after another; let us therefore, Madam, said I— Here she interrupted me bawling as loud as she could hollow; Nothing, nothing will make amends for the stain you have brought upon my family and the reputation of the young lady. The young Lady! quoth I, very young forsooth; may I chew my whiskers if she is not as old as the Mamaluke of Egypt who has been on the throne above an hundred years. Young or old, replied she, if you don't instantly make her amends by giving her your hand in wedlock, I'll call for the watch and send you to the work house. Wedlock, wedlock, said I, why in the name of sense and reason would you have me marry a Witch. Marry her! yes, replied she, and you may live very happily with her too; her experience join'd to your boyish ignorance will carry you merrily thro' the world. Hold, hold madam, quoth I, you will as soon persuade me to swallow my boots whole as to marry a whore, a Gipsey, a witch or something worse; here is my purse if that will satisfy you; it shall be at your service; so saying I handed it to her; it was made of bear's skin the flesh side out; it contained a couple of two-shilling pieces, a five penny bit, a yard of Pigtail Tobacco, a tooth picker and an english shilling, which notwithstanding their value I was willing to part with to purchase peace: but she had no sooner saw them than she fell at me again crying, Zounds what does the brute mean, can you imagine I regard your vile trash? Hey! is this the person we took for a gentleman; have you nothing better than these; where is your watch, let us have that, produce the watch, the watch. The watch! Madam, for Mahomet's sake, have patience a moment and, and— No, no, said she, I don't mean to call the watch upon you yet; I'll have my ends out of you first; I mean your pocket watch, hand us that. Upon my honour Madam, said I, I have none, nor ever had in my life; but pray restrain your passion, and I will give you something more valuable, than a score of watches. What's that, said she? Here, here, said I, pulling out an old manuscript wrote by a Jewish Cabalist, a lock of Peter the hermit's whiskers and the 10th part of Mahomet's beard; these valuable reliques which I esteem next my life, will certainly satisfy you. At this she began to rave, stamp, and swear like a madwoman, and calling up the bully mentioned before, he and the hostler taking me by the heels, drew me down stairs, tumbled me into the street and hurled my Turban, my purse and my staff after me in the greatest confusion. I was now in a confounded pickle, without house or home exposed to the evils of a dark night; however I was resolved to put the best face on it that I could, and hereupon I again equipped myself in my usual mode and took to the street intending to depart from this dangerous and heathenish city. But as I was making the best of my way out, the hollow tread of my feet gave notice to the watchmen, who immediately came in pursuit of me; as I was entangled by my boots I should certainly have been caught had not my good stars directed me to a yard full of cattle; here I made up to a barrack of hay, which was standing at the upper end of the yard, and laid myself down in it and no sooner had I fell asleep but I dreamed, that I saw an ox of an enormous size, approaching me to chew my Jacket, boots, wallet, and Turban; when I awoke in the morning I found it but too true, for my wallet was almost tore to pieces and my Jacket and purse were chewed entirely up. I was almost distracted for the loss of the reliques, but as the day was advancing I found I had no time to lose, so immediately packing up my remaining articles, I made down to the port where the ships rose like forests on the waves; here I ran up and down the Quay enquiring for Commodore Russel, but instead of an answer one gave me a damn, a 2^d a box on the Ear and a 3^d a kick on the Breech; at last I met with the Commodore himself. But the conference I had with him and some particulars relative to our voyage, I shall treat of in the next chapter.

IL
[Hugh Brackenridge]

Chapter 2ᵈ

Arma virumque cano &c.

VIRG.

Arms and the man I sing who forced by fate
And haughty Juno's unrelenting hate
Expell'd and exil'd left his native shore
Long Labours both by land and sea he bore.

No sooner had I met the Commodore than he burst out into a loud horse laugh, saluting me thus: Father Bombo how goes it with you? how have you done this long time, which way are you steering? Steering Sir! replied I, can you possibly be ignorant that I am on the point of sailing with you to Africa? But pray, when do you set off? I intend to weigh anchor, said he, at nine o'Clock tomorrow morning and you shall be highly welcome to accompany me as we are old Companions and Messmates. Thank you Sir, said I, I will be on board precisely at the time appointed. And where do you intend to tarry in the mean time, said he? I cannot positively answer that, replied I, but a crotchet has just come into my head to take a turn up to King's college, and I am sure I shall be well received by the students, as I am a scholar myself and have been brought up one. Ay, ay, said he, do just as your own mind directs you, only remember to be here at the time appointed. I quickly left the Commodore and hastened away to the college where I arrived in little more than half an hour. I found that the building, which was truly grand, was surrounded with a spacious board-fence, painted red: in one side of it was a large gate which I found fast shut; at first I attempted to open it with my hand, but finding that was vain I bethought myself of another expedient; I retreated from the gate about 30 yards, then holding my staff in an horizontal direction horned end fore-most, I gave the gate such a shock that it opened so easily, that I

45

flew thro' it head foremost without being able to stop myself and plow'd up a small quantity of earth with my nose; this immediately excited a violent laugh from the students who were looking out of their windows. Enraged at this, I jumped up and cryed as I advanced towards the college, Ah young Masters! you don't do well to laugh at persons in distress; such misfortunes will happen to all. This did but increase their laughter, and especially as they knew they had nothing to fear from me. I resolved, however, to restrain my rage; because I knew should we come to an engagement the Odds of the battle would be to my sorrow. I therefore put on a smiling countenance and advanced up to the great middle door. As soon as I entered it I took towards a room which lay on my left hand, but in the way tarred a wall prodigiously with my Turban, for which one of the officers of the house reprimanded me severely, and threatened to turn me out of the house if I did not take more pains for the future. Ay, please your worship, said I, that's well spoke; a word to the wise is enough. I then traversed the College and at length determined to enter a chamber where I saw several young Gentlemen, talking and smoking over a glass of wine; I accordingly essayed to enter the door, but my Turban absolutely refused, for it was above two feet higher than the top of the door. The students seeing the perplexity I was in, immediately rose up and one of them supplanting my heels, brought me on my back in an instant; then seizing me by the straps of the boots, they hauled me in, with no other damage done to me than discomposing my Turban a little. I observed all this time, they endeavoured to restrain their laughter, lest, as I apprehended, they should have provoked me to anger. After I was introduced in this comical manner, they desired me to sit down in a large elbow chair. Gentlemen, said I, I am afraid I am a great trouble to you, but, without interrupting your learned discourse, I beg leave to ask, whether you have breakfasted yet. Breakfasted! answered one, yes, three hours ago; it is now, continued he, pulling out his watch, Eleven o'Clock and so far from breakfasting that we begin to think of dining. Ay, answered I, is it so then, very well, I ask pardon for the interruption I have given you, I only asked on account of my belly which growls dreadfully and seems to hint it is breakfast time there, let it be when it will with you; however as you say dinner time is approaching I will use my endeavours to restrain my gnawing appetite. Fire and fury, replied one of them, who the Devil sent you here, you voracious Glutton; is this a place for you to stuff your confounded guts which the Devil grant may send you into a thousand pieces the moment you get out of the gate. Being highly offended I started up, being hardly able to speak a word thro' vexation and hunger, and brandishing my staff would have slain the presumptuous youth that very moment, had not the others interpos'd, at whose request I spared his life. After this they shewed me more respect than before and we talked very freely upon various learned topics 'till the bell rung for dinner, when I was desired to walk down with them; this offer I gladly accepted and put in execution, getting thro' the door as when I came in. When we arrived at the dining room they all crowded up in a hurry to the upper end of the table and left me to shift for myself at the very tail of the Company. Blood and Butcher-knives! said I, to myself, I shall not be able to get a single mouthful here. As soon as the Grace was said, they fell to most voraciously and loaded their plates in an instant, with the most savoury food I had smelt this long time; I say smelt, for as yet there was no possibility of my taking a morsel, it being entirely out of my reach. At last I asked one who sat next me if he thought there was any moral probability of my getting any thing to eat; in return, he only laughed at me and said I should have looked out in Time. Time! said I, why I have been trying for an opportunity to get a slash ever since I sat down and have not been able to get a toothful; he replied he had no time to spare in talking; so there I sat like a fool with my empty plate. This treatment, together with the instigation of my belly, so inraged

47

me that I sprang up with my knife and fork, leaped quite over the table, and rushed up to the head, where seeing a fine dish of roasted beef and potatoes, I made but one cut and had above three parts of it suspended by my fork and teeth, for by reason of the weight, the fork alone was not strong enough to hold it; in this manner I ran down, sprang over the table again to my place where I found my plate in the hands of a young student, which I recovered by giving him a blow with my fist which laid him sprawling on the floor; and what is very surprizing, all this was done to the great surprize of the Vice-president and tutors who sat at the upper end of the table. To make short of the matter: I finished my repast to my great Content and spent the whole afternoon in learned discourses with the students. In the Evening I supped with them and afterwards at my request, I was lodged in a spacious room in the upper story, but in the morning to my great surprize found myself lying in a dry ditch near two miles from the city. This the rascals had done while I slept. I thought it beneath me to repay such creatures in their own Coin, otherwise I would not have left one stone of the College upon another. I now packed up and advancing thro' the town, repassed the College and hastened to the dock; by this time it was past Nine o'Clock and all that detained the Commodore was myself only; as soon as he saw me at the dock he sent off his barge from the ship which was getting under sail, and I was instantly fetched on board. The Commodore welcomed me to the Ship and ordered a sailor to shew me my birth to which I descended by means of a ladder. I found it to be in the steerage; here I immediately deposited my wallet and locked the door and ascended on deck. The sails were all hoisted and we scudded before the wind with amazing velocity, so that we soon lost sight of the City, and that same evening we came to anchor off of sandy hook which is the entrance into the Ocean. But a brisk gale springing up about midnight we weighed Anchor and put off to sea.

We sailed without any remarkable adventure for ten days except that I was made Captain of the Watch, this office obliging me to ly on Deck all night. I had a good opportunity of viewing the stars; and as I had studied astronomy it was a good amusement in my vacant time. Here one night as I was attentively considering the planets I saw Orion arise and a black speck appear on the tail of the Cod-fish; at this I was extremely terrified and immediately prognosticated an approaching storm, but was told by the seamen that there was no danger; however I composed the following song which shall conclude this chapter:

I

Reclin'd upon the deck I lay
And heard the roaring of the sea;
Black was the gloom of night and dark the shade;
The feeble notes of fairy bands
That fly on clouds from distant lands
Alarm'd my fears as we press'd oer the watry glade.

2

I watch'd the stars and midnight skies,
I saw the watry Orion rise
And lift his glitt'ring head above the deep,
Where in Tithonus' seats below
The murmuring waves forever blow
And lull the drowsy God to everlasting sleep.

3

Sure Sign of storms and blust'ring gales
To swell the deep and tear our sails
O Star! so baleful! sink thy head again!
O let your weary Sailors rest!
O stay forever in the East
Nor rear thy dreaded face above the western main.

4

Yet cease from fear my dauntless mind
Despite the Tempests and the wind,
Nor tremble at old Ocean's distant roar;
I fear no Tempests winds or storms
Nor death in all its various forms
While wafted safely by the Commodore.

JΓ

[Philip Freneau]

Chapter 3ᵈ

We jolly men passing over the Sea
For certain causes into a far countrie.

CHAUCER

The Welkin clear and the seven stars yestreen
Sliding far down in the west right smoothly were seen
While far from the land full merrily we
Alongst with each other plough'd the deep sea.

SPENSER

Permit me to introduce the following part of my story with the old tho' just observation, "that those who sail on board the same ship may be said to ly in the same belly," or to stretch the allusion farther, may be said to live in the same house and as we on board the Commodore's ship stood in the relation of a family to one another, it will be expected that I being acquainted with the crew should give a particular description of the most remarkable persons on board; this therefore shall be the subject of this chapter. And here I shall begin with Jeffery Slyboots the chaplain; Jeffery was a Scotchman, born in the town of Kilmarnock and educated at the College of Aberdeen; he was a very jolly fellow, could take a bowl and crack a Jest now and then as well as the best of us, as most Chaplains can do. Jeffery from our first interview, behaved himself extremely well towards me, rightly judging that by doing so he would please the Commodore with whom I was in high repute. The next most remarkable personage on board was Brocado the Commodore's brother; Brocado was as valiant a fellow as ever handled cold Iron. The Commodore took him on board because he understood Greek and might be of service to him in trading among the Greeks of the Archipelagian Islands; this barber was a very knowing fellow, he could talk of Politicks like a Coffee-house statesman, he knew the names of all the kings and Princes in Europe, dictated all the Commodore's letters and thus served him in a double capacity of Barber and Scrivener. The next remarkable person was the Boatswain; his proper name was Thomas Holliwood, but in his youth having been bound to a Soap boiler and ill used by his master, he ran away and changed his name to that of Hector Goodchuck. Some years afterwards being pressed by a privateer, he gave them the slip as they were taking in water somewhere on the coast of England and changed his name to that of Huron O'Boyne. Now being reduced by poverty he led a retired life in Badnor shire in Wales, 'till one night coming to the town of Slandaff without any money in his pocket and scarcely any cloaths to his back he was taken up for a shop-lifter and the next day when he was brought before Dafah Thomas John the Mayor, considering that Huron Boyne was a suspicious name he changed it to Taffy ap Jones and putting on a very simple face, passing for an honest Welchman he got off clear, having first bribed the Mayor with a couple pounds of Cheese which he got conveyed privately to him the night before. After this he travelled by land to Liverpool; there he met with the Commodore and passing for a sailor, he engaged in his service, and now resolving to become a new man he divested himself of all his fictitious names retaining only that of Conrad Cor, which is the name by which he now passes. Conrad piqued himself much on his abilities as an Orator; he had a great flow of words, some masterly gestures and strokes of hand, and had such a command of himself that he could cry, sing and whistle all in the same breath, which I take to be the quintessence of Oratory. The Commodore's lady likewise deserves to be mentioned by me as she was my very good friend thro' the Voyage, that is, she was serviceable in common respects but not otherwise. I might just give a hint that Aliborah the Skipper was aboard and his character you heard before; I might likewise tell you of Benjamin Guzzle the Cooke, Will Wimble the Mate and many others, but for Brevity shall pass on to relate some disasters that befell me and which I look upon as inseparable from the Character of a Pilgrim. One day as the Chaplain, Commodore and myself were walking on deck, the Chaplain broke silence in this manner: Commodore, said he, it is by no means a mark of good œconomy to suffer this Pilgrim of ours to keep Nineteen or Twenty ells of Linnen folded on his head, like a Webb on a Weaver's beam, when if a Storm should overtake us and tear away our Mainsail this Turban of his would supply their place excellently well. A good thought, upon my word, said the Commodore, it will make excellent staying to the main shrouds; Ay, or to trace the Halyards, said Slyboots. Gentlemen, said I, you all know the design of my voyage and it would be utterly inconsistent to appear as a Pilgrim without a Turban among Mohametans. Besides suppose I could make shift to do without it were I ashore, yet I must have a head dress on sea. Ay, ay, said the Chaplain, that's very true, but here's Brocado the Barber; he'll make you a Wig in two hours time. A Wig Gentlemen! said I, I cannot in character wear one. Not a word more, said the Commodore, by the Trident of Neptune, you shall have a Wig; for I cannot do without the Turban. Call up Brocado, let us see if he will engage to make him a Wig. Here, Mr. Brocado, continued the Commodore, can you make Father Bombo a Wig? Yes, please your Worship, I believe I could fit the Gentleman to a nicety, but stay: Let me see what colour will suit him. Let me view the first Bush of his Physiognomy. I'll make him a Wig as light as vanity, as jim as a Soliloquy, as round, as smooth, as complete, as a Burlesque. Well, well, says the Commodore, what colour then do you say will suit him? Why let me see: his Complexion is sanguine, I think a red Wig will be the very plan. A red Wig, said the Chaplain, no, no, let him have one the colour of his Eyebrows. A grey one would be much the best. If I might speak my mind between you both, said the Commodore, I would chuse a white Wig for my friend Bombo. But that a point of such importance may be fully settled,

53

let every man freely offer his reasons for the colour he proposes, and we will call down Conrad Cor the Boatswain, and Aliborah the Skipper to be judges in this nice affair. Conrad and Aliborah being accordingly come Slyboots the Chaplain stood forth and spoke thus:

Gentlemen,

The Poets have made use of a grey colour as an Epithet of the morning, for what is more common than to hear them say,

> The sober twilight in his dusky grey?

You will likewise observe that a grey hound is the swiftest in the chace and moreover it was a grey goose that saved the Roman Capitol from besieging Gauls by her cackling as the poet expresses it:

> _____ 'Twas a Grey Goose
> That kept the Capitol and watchful sav'd
> The Roman Empire from besieging Gauls.

It is with a grey goose quill that the lover expresses the tender Emotions of his heart to his absent fair one, and it was an arrow feather'd with grey that shot Earl Douglass in the battle of chevy-chase, as is evident from the following lines:

> The grey-goose wing that was therein
> In his heart's blood was wet.

These, Gentlemen, are my reasons for a Grey Wig.

Then the Commodore spoke in favour of a white one in the following manner:

The chaplain, I must confess, has spoke very learnedly but I think a white colour is to be preferred to grey. White was a mark of distinction among the Romans; the Senator's robes were white, and the beans by which they absolved Criminals are white. Milk white steeds is an Epithet truly poetic and moreover white is an emblem of chastity; Shakespear was convinced of this when he said his wife was,

> Chaste as the unsun'd snow,

and what can be whiter than snow; but if I needed any thing to strengthen these reasons, I might add that white was held as an Omen of good luck in all ages and places. 'Twas a white heifer Cadmus saw when he founded the city of Thebes; 'twas a white sow that taught Eneas to call his city Alba or white and a white Elephant is at this day worshipped by the Persians and finally the Turbans among the Turks are white and therefore a white Wig will gain the more credit among them.

Then the Barber began his speech in favour of a red Wig as follows:

A red wig is by far the most commodious as it will suit the colour of his beard which was singed red at his first setting out. It is also honourable; the flag of England is red, the blush of the morning is red, the rose on a lady's cheek is red. The Persians worship the fire and the fire is red; the full moon is red, every thing noble and lively is red, the vital drops of blood are red. Therefore I think a red Wig will become him best. But what I think will fairly determine it on my side is this; I have neither Wool, Tow, or Hair of any colour but red on board and therefore you must take what I have. When the Barber had made an end of his speech the Boatswain and Skipper desired him, since that was the case, to construct one to his own liking with all imaginable Dexterity. In two days' time the Wig was finished and when put on the curls came dangling down to the waistband of my boots. My circumstances were now very happy and would have continued so had not the fury of my destiny prevented it by the following unlucky affair.

The evening after I had got my wig, as I was walking along the Gangway, I met the Commodore's Lady and thinking this a fit opportunity to give her the Beveridge of my wig, I went to kiss her at which she screamed out and raised the whole crew upon me. The Commodore immediately starting up upon Deck hoisted me up to the halyards and ordered Conrad Cor to lash me half an hour with a rope's end. After I had continued a long time in this unmerciful situation, the Commodore ordered me down to be clapped into a hog's head, nailed up and thrown overboard. Accordingly I was instantly put into a hogshead and bunged up so close that I could see niether sun, moon or stars; four Sailors took me up and had me on the Gunwale of the ship ready as soon as the word of Command was given to tumble me into the Sea. But now my melancholy situation moved the pity of Slyboots the Chaplain, so that he wheedled the Commodore down into the Cabbin to take a bowl of Grog before my execution and in the mean time the Skipper and Boatswain promised the sailors a Bottle of Burgundy apiece if they would save my Life; hereupon they rolled me down into the hold and substituted another hogshead in my place, which, upon the Commodore's return was kicked overboard and followed by three cheers from the ship. Ah, said he, there goes Bombo! As jolly a fellow as ever I knew and one for whom I had the greatest respect, 'till the Devil put it into his head to tempt my wife from her duty. Here I lay in the hold, fixed up in the hogshead, having nothing to do but sucking my fingers, like a bear having nothing else to live on. Sometime after when the Commodore became more pacified and his passion subsided, he repented of the hasty sentence he had passed upon me. In short he could get no rest Day or night, like Alexander, when he killed his friend Clitus. But the Skipper now finding it a seasonable time, told him the whole Joke; hereupon he leaped out of the Cabbin like one transported; ordered me to be hoisted up on deck and the End knocked out of the hogshead. I immediately sprung out as alert as a Roebuck, embraced the Commodore, washed my beard, had my Wig powdered and sat down by his side. The bowls circulated around, healths and

toasts flowed apace and everything put on the appearance of mer-
riment and security. The Commodore desired me to sing a song
on this happy Occasion, upon which I struck up the following
chorus:

1

The air is calm, the Welkin clear;
By Newfoundland our ship we steer,
Bound for Barbary's sandy shore;
Here's a health to our noble Commodore.

2

While yonder stars surround the poles
Let's send about our flowing bowls
And drive away our griefs encore;
Success to our gallant Commodore.

IL
[Hugh Brackenridge]

Chapter 4th

Explebo numerum, reddarque tenebris.

ENEID 6 v. 545

The number I'll fulfill and to the shades retire.

We were now advanced 600 Leagues on our Voyage and consequently more than half way towards our desired port; it being however now three weeks since we left the land I began to be exceeding weary of this kind of life and especially as I had that strange disease they call sea-sickness, insomuch that I had not the least satisfaction in eating, drinking, or sleeping, for after I had dined I was sure to throw up my whole repast in a quarter of an hour and this was always the case, whether I was awake or asleep, during the whole voyage. In other respects I lived very happy, being restored both to the favour of the Commodore and his lady. But nevertheless, the Devil who is at the root of all evil would not let me rest, but persuaded me one night, to get up and put all the Ships crew in Irons, that I might have her in my own possession and go wherever I pleased. My plan was, to steer round the cape of good hope thro' the Indian Ocean into the red sea and so arrive at Mecca without the trouble of walking or burning my feet on the hot sands of Africa. I accordingly roused myself and put my plan in execution without delay; I first armed myself with my staff and then marching softly to the steerage, bound every rascally sailor aboard, hand and foot, so that they could scarcely stir one way or another; after I had finished this exploit I stepped to the Cabbin and bound the Commodore in Irons; the rest I fast'ned with ropes. When I came to the priest's birth, I found him wide awake, and when I was going to bind his legs, he bawled out, Who in the name of Beelzebub have we here? As I was now on the point of being discovered, I clapped the Spike of my staff to his breast and whispered: "Hold your tongue you rascall or by my wig I will transfix you this moment like a Goose on a Spit"; this resolute speech obliged him to silence and I bound his Arms and legs with the greatest ease; I then mounted on Deck and having discharged my supper overboard by means of my mouth, I took the helm and steered the course I intended which was not difficult for me as I had studied Navigation and Geography. As we had a fine gale, I ran the ship right before it and went with a surprizing rapidity. The moon shone very bright, by which means I saw a large vessel at some distance making directly towards me. Bless me! said I to myself, what shall I do; if these are Pirates they will certainly take the ship and put me to death as I am not able to manage the Guns; but on the other hand if I loose the Commodore and men, they will surely secure me and in all probability after being tryed by a Court-martial, I shall be hung up at the yard arm without benefit of clergy. While I was reflecting in this manner the other ship bore down to me and as soon as they were near enough halloed in the Spanish language to this Effect. Ho, whence are you and whither are you bound? At this I jumped up and pulling off my bootbreeches replied thus to them. I am a Pilgrim travelling to Mecca and if you give me any of your Insolence I will fire a broadside and sink you in a moment. This they heard and finding themselves treated with so little ceremony, fired a 36 pounder at me; however the damage I received was very inconsiderable, having no more than a lock of my wig taken off as it grazed my head; roused by their intolerable impudence, I fired three guns at them and as I have since heard killed as many persons. I then veered off as fast as I was able and they pursued, but as our ship was the better sailor I lost sight of them in an hour's time. But I forgot to tell you that the report of the guns waked the Commodore who, when he found himself tyed fast, roared out, who in the world has had the impudence to serve me thus? Ay, replied the Chaplain, who could hardly speak for pain, you do well to ask that, but pray ask your Friend Mr. Bombo. Bombo, said the

Commodore? Sir, says I; who has tyed us up in this manner? said he. No matter, Sir, returned I, don't make yourself uneasy in the least; you shall be loosed in about six weeks or whenever I reach my intended port; in the mean time I will supply you and all the crew with those necessaries you will have occasion for, provided you do not behave in an insolent manner toward me. I then continued my course two whole days, 'till at length one of the Seamen by some cursed mishap, broke his shackles and loosed himself from his confinement; then he untyed another and they two, stepping upon deck, made towards me with great fury, intending to seize me; while lifting up my staff, I attempted to knock the brains out of one of them, but, unhappily for me, missed my stroke, which came full drive upon the pump and left the fellows at liberty and put me in Irons, which they no sooner had done, than clapping a tackle to my Wig and boots they lowered me into the hold, leaving me to lament my cruel destiny; I passed away my time in the most melancholy reflections concerning my punishment and in the meantime the Sailors who secured me, unbound the men; and then the Commodore, Chaplain and other persons of note, meeting in the great Cabbin, consulted together concerning the heinous crime I had committed and it was resolved that I should be tried next day by a court martial exactly at Nine o'Clock in the morning; but the Commodore falling ill it was postponed a week longer, by which time we were within 300 miles of the town of Algiers, our intended port. When the time for my trial came at last, I was ordered to be brought on deck, having my Wig powdered and boots cleaned. As soon as I was brought forth I found the quarter deck was appointed to be the scene of trial. The Commodore sat in a large Elbow chair as chief Judge, Brocado was clerk, Conrad Cor they appointed for my counsel, the Skipper was the Second justice, Slyboots was king's attorney and Benjamin Guzzle his Assistant; as for Will Wimble he was cryer. Besides these there were twelve Sailors appointed for Jurymen to bring in their verdict when the trial was over. Thus all things being ready I was clapped into an Oblong box which when it stood on end reached about the middle of my breast; this was the barr. Then the Clerk produced the following accusations on paper which he read:

You Reynardine Bombo late of the continent of America, have been detected and seized in the very perpetration of one of the most horrid crimes that ever lodged in a human breast, in endeavouring to turn Pirate and betray our right honourable Commander, the ship and all of us into the hands of the Turks. This you stand indicted for at this tribunal and you are required to declare yourself guilty or not Guilty of the crime herein specified. When this question was put I at first had some thoughts of answering it in the negative but finding the fact so indisputably plain, I had not the face to do it and so confessed Guilty. But, continued I, what signifies it whether I am guilty or not; I think you are shamefull guilty of only giving me bread and water to eat these ten days. By my boots and wig, unless my stomach is immediately satisfied, I'll not answer you a word and try what you can do with me then. At these words, which were spoken in a very resolute manner, the Commodore ordered a luncheon of Pork on deck, which I had no sooner laid hands on, than I devoured, and ever since that time I have loved pork better than any kind of Beef whatever. After I had swallowed the pork I cryed out not guilty. What does the fellow say, replied the Commodore; he says he is not guilty, answered the Clerk. Ay, and are you not guilty then, you scoundrel, said the Commodore, and will you force us to prove it? Yes faith will I, said I, with great spirit, and I guess you'll find hard work to do it too. Well, said the Clerk, who will you be tried by, your king or country? Ay that's well thought of, replied I, by my country, by all means. Then the Clerk called the Jury over one by one and after he found all present, the witnesses were summoned to appear, which were the two sailors who secured me in the hold. They asked the first one a question thus: What know you of the conspiracy of that vile rascal Bombo? Pray Sir, interrupted I, is it the fashion, in your court partials as you call them, to call people upon trial villain and rascals? if so I think you are partial with a witness. No sooner had I spoke thus than the clerk gave me a most violent stroke over the head and ordered me to hold my tongue instantly, or I should be hung up without Judge or Jury. Then the Witness began his narrative thus: May it please your worships I found myself waked out of sleep with the pain which the ropes gave me with which I was bound by this villain; in this condition I lay several hours 'till by struggling and good luck I got one of my arms loose, which slipping into my pocket I drew out my knife and cut the other ropes; I then loosed my comrade and we both quickly sprung upon deck and found Reynardine steering where he pleased without controul. We immediately concluded that he had been the Author of the mischief on board and accordingly seized him as before mentioned, and laid him in the hold where he has remained 'till your honours thought fit to deliver him from the same in order for his tryal. The deposition of the other witness was to the same purport. When these things appeared so plain the Commodore asked me if I had any thing to say in defence of myself. I answered no, but relied on his mercy. Ah, said he, you do very foolishly to put yourself in my power twice running. Then the Jury having brought me in guilty the Clerk stood up and read my sentence, which was this: "That you Reynardine Bombo be carried to the place from whence you came and from thence be dragged by two sailors to the foremast of the vessel and be hanged up at the yard arm." When this was read, I bowed down my head and desired the favour to be hung in my Wig and boots. This they assented to and I was immediately remanded back to prison, where, as soon as I arrived, I writ a letter to the Commodore and begged him that I might be reprieved two days longer, that I might read something out of the Alcoran suitable to the season. This was also granted and I fell to it very heartily and in the intervals the chaplain used to visit me and exhort me to bear with patience my hard fortune and not to be terrified in the least as this had ruined the Reputation of many great men who had hanged before me. Well, Sir, said I, but would you not be terrified if you were in my situation? That's a thing that at present I cannot satisfy you in, replied he, and so left me. However I kept in good spirits 'till the word was given to hoist me on Deck in order for execution; then I was hauled by two sailors on a sledge to the forepart of the vessel and mounted on a high scaffold hung upon this Occasion by slings; then a rope was put around my neck, the other end whereof reached to the Top Gallant sail yard. Bless me! said I, I shall be swung high enough if that will do. Then the Cryer informed me that by the favour of the commodore the Chaplain was allowed to preach a sermon before I was turned off. This I thanked them for but begged leave in the first place to read my Will, as follows:

Mr. Bombo's last Will and Testament—

In the Name of Mahomet, Amen. I Reynardine Bombo at present a Pilgrim travelling to Mecca, finding it suitable to my present circumstances not to live any longer, do in consequence thereof make this my last will and Testament, declaring all other writings of this kind, void and of no Effect. Imprimis: I bequeath half a pound of Tobacco to the Commodore to make use of to remember me. Item: half a dozen pipes to the Chaplain, together with my Alcoran; as for my manuscripts in my wallet I leave them to Aliborah the skipper hoping he will print them shortly after my decease. Item: my dictionaries to Conrad Cor, which I need not tell him are double their first value by reason of the explanatory notes which I have inserted almost in every leaf. Item: Peter the hermit to the Commodore's lady which I am sure will be an acceptable Legacy as I have observed she is somewhat religious. My Wig I leave to Will Wimble as I have heard him frequently say he wanted one but had not money enough to purchase it. Whatever else I am worth, I leave to Benjamin Guzzle in gratitude for his having supply'd me with victuals and drink while in prison. This, Gentlemen, is my whole Estate and you see I have equally disposed of it among my friends. All I now desire, is, that you would be careful to get this last adventure of my life bound up with the rest that the world may see the uncertainty of human life, even in the most smiling and prosperous condition. But lastly I hereby constitute the Commodore and Chaplain executors to this my Will, hoping they will take due care to deliver the legacies to the persons specified.

Signed, Sealed, and deliver'd in the presence of

Benjamin Guzzle ⎫   *Reynardine Bombo*
                          ⎬ Witnesses
Will Wimble   ⎭   L. S.

As soon as I had finished reading this they all burst out into a hideous laugh and cryed out that this will of mine might as well have continued in a state of nonexistence, as they intended to throw my wallet into the sea after myself when I was hanged. At these words I bowed my head and said, the will of Mahomet be done. Then the Priest preach'd his discourse, the most of which at the time, I took down in short hand for curiosity's sake. The substance of it follows:

The Sermon of Mr. Jeffery Slyboots preached at the Execution of Mr. Reynardine Bombo.

Gentlemen,

The subject of the following discourse you will find recorded in the 3^d ode of the 2^d book of the renowned poet Horace:

Æquam memento, rebus in arduis
Servare mentem; non secus in bonis
Ab insolenti temparatam
Lætitia, Moriture Bombo.

In arduous things an equal mind maintain
Nor let your spirit rise too high
Tho' fortune kindly change the scene
Alas! O Bombo, thou wert born to die.

The former clause of the verse I purpose to chiefly insist upon
as most adapted to the present occasion, as it contains advice to
persons in adversity. Adversity is that galling slavish chain which
makes every evil appear in its most terrible supernatural colours.
Consider, Father Bombo, and reflect with Joy on the many con-
solatory passages you have lately read in the Alcoran suitable
to your present circumstances and on the other hand look back
with Terror on the heinous and aggravated crimes you have been
guilty of and which have brought you to this shameful end and
then consider what my text advises you to, Viz: "Not to be cast
down in adversity," and I am persuaded you will think no more
of hanging here half an hour or so, than to get up in the night
and put the ship's crew in fetters. But to return to my text, I
would now propose several things to your serious consideration
which may lighten your heavy affliction. In the first place what
can be more desirable to a person in your situation than to be
rid of a life which is made up of nothing but troubles and bad
luck; I am sure any charitable person that reads your history will
lament that you live so long only to be buffeted by the boisterous
waves of adverse fortune. Add to this: if you were not now to be
hanged, you would be forced to undergo numberless fatigues in
your long Journey over the desarts of Lybia and especially as
you have no shoes fit for any human creature. Ay, faith, interrupted I, but I have boots tho'. This speech set them all a
laughing, 'till the Chaplain proceeded thus: Secondly, in your
Journey over vast Desarts, I am positive your wallet would not
be half sufficient to supply you with provisions; even suppose
you would take out your Dictionaries, the consequence is plain;
you would starve with hunger and die without the benefit of a

Sermon. The Devil thank you for your Sermon, quoth I softly, I wish it was ended. Thirdly, your being hanged here will entirely absolve you from your vow of Pilgrimage; for neither Mahomet nor Lucian can expect a Journey of 4 or 5000 miles to be performed by a dead man. Fourthly and lastly, we have hardly enough of provisions on board to serve the crew a week longer and unless we reach our intended port by that time, I know not what we shall do. This shall suffice as the doctrinal part of my subject, showing the necessity we are under of hanging you immediately; I now proceed to the Application. You all are sensible from what has been said that Mr. Bombo is under no terrors on account of his suspension from the yard-arm; I therefore think it will be very proper to swing him off immediately, while he continues in this temper of mind, for I am positive I could not bring him to the same key again were I to preach 'till midnight. Therefore wishing him a good Journey I say Amen and Amen. Hold your Worship, roared I, it is certainly always the privilege of Pilgrims, to sing a hymn before they are turned off. The priest then informed me, there was neither bible nor Psalm book aboard and therefore they could not gratify my request. Ay, replied I, but by good fortune I lately composed one suitable for the present Occasion, as I expected it would happen; I will therefore read it off line by line and I beg you would do me the favour, Mr. Wimble, to set the Tune; he accordingly cleared his throat and set the tune of the black Joke to the following verses:

> The lagging hour at last is come
> To seal my last, my final doom,
> These are the dire Effects of Lucian's rage;
> So are the flow'rs of winter nipt,
> Ah! curse that fatal manuscript
> That sent me on this wretched Pilgrimage.

While here suspended by a rope,
That bane of ev'ry future hope,
I like a crow must dangle in the Sky;
Yet let me bid a long adieu
To Wimble, Guzzle and to you
That round my neck the fatal cord doth tye.

As soon as the hymn was concluded the hangman climbed up to the main Halyards, in order to turn me off the scaffold. My Wig was pulled over my eyes and he was waiting for the signal of execution, when Mahomet interposed in my favour and caused the hangman to spy a large ship about 3 leagues ahead bearing down upon us full sail; this we could not perceive before as all hands were sitting under a canopy of Canvas in order for my trial. The Hangman never minding me instantly told the Commodore that a large Palacca under french colours was bearing upon us ahead; this roused them all to the engagement and in the hurry of clearing the Decks and pulling the ropes tight in order to bring the ship to bear I was hoisted together with my scaffold, almost to the main top mast, where I sat as contentedly with my wallet on my back as if nothing had been the matter. At last the Frenchman came within gun shot and gave us a furious Broadside, which compliment the Commodore instantly returned and a desperate engagement ensued which lasted near two hours greatly to the disadvantage of our Commodore, who at last was obliged to surrender and ordered me to strike the colours, as I and my scaffold were within reach of them. This I did with such dexterity amidst a storm of Bullets and grape shot which whistled about my Ears, that it perfectly charmed the French Captain who was resolved to make me his own at any rate. After we had struck he sent his barge to bring the Commodore aboard his ship, where he stayed several hours while near on half of the Enemy boarded us to prevent our running away. At last the

Commodore returned and told us he had ransomed the Ship at a great price and that I was part of it. What the Devil, said I, must I be sold about like a Negro; no, by my wig I'll assert the rights of Pilgrims be where I will. Scarcely had I spoke these words when the Frenchman sent his barge for the ransom money immediately as he was in haste, being homeward bound. Then the Commodore lowered a large box of money into the boat and giving me a hearty kick on the breech sent me after it full drive, insulting me with this unmanly and brutish speech, Go, you Dog, you rascal and thank your stars that you have escaped hanging so easily. I then left the Commodore's Ship without much regret as any one may well suppose after hearing my adventures there. We were now in sight of the pillars of Hercules which by observation we found to be 12 leagues distant; I then saw the Commodore make the best of his way thro' the straits of Gibraltar, while we steered northward towards the bay of Biscay, designing to sail up the River Seyne to Paris the Capital of old France. My new French master used me exceeding well, on account of my activity and address in quality of Cabbin Boy, and assured me that when we arrived at Paris, I should have the choice either of attending him in future Voyages in some honourable post, or to go ashore and stay in the city, where, he said, he doubted not but I should be speedily advanced on account of my extraordinary merit. Thus, I spent my time on board as merry as a cricket and used well by every one, so that you may see—

Great blessings always wait on virtuous deeds
And tho' a late, a sure reward succeeds.

JΓ
[Philip Freneau]

The End of the Second Book.

68

Father Bombo's Pilgrimage to Mecca

Book the Third

Preface to Book 3ᵈ

The Editors of this work think fit to acquaint him or those who shall read this history, that we designed to comprize the whole in the three present books; but several intervening circumstances concurring to hinder our prosecution of our design at large, we have concluded in as hasty a manner as possible, tho' perhaps, too abruptly, which defect we hope our readers (if we have any) will pardon, as also some mistakes both in Grammar and Stile, which insensibly crept in as we proceeded along, this being the first draught, warm from the brain, and it was impossible to correct it, without more blotting and interlineations, than we would willingly chuse to insert.

JΓ and IL
[Philip Freneau and
Hugh Brackenridge]

————— Mutato nomine
Fabula de te narratur.

HOR

——— Change but the name
The story's told of you.

Chapter 1st

Integer vitæ, scelerisque purus
Non eget Mauri, Jaculis neque arcu
Nec venenatis, gravida Sagittis
          Fusce Pharetra

Sive per Syrtes Iter æstuosas
Sive facturus, per inhospitalem
Caucasum, vel quæ, loca fabulosus
          Lambit Hydaspes

HORACE

The man who keeps his conscience clear
Shall neither swords nor daggers fear
Nor barbed arrows shot from Parthian bows,
     Not tho' he wanders in all lands
     Or stears his course thro' burning sands
In which some poison'd river flows.

IL
[Hugh Brackenridge]

The name of the french captain, who took the Commodore, was Monsieur de Pivot; he appeared to be a very brave and worthy Gentleman, and I began to promise myself very happy days in the sunshine of his Favour, especially as he was an extravagant lover of the polite arts and I a great Connoiseur in them; but all my fine hopes were blasted by a surprizing instance of the ups and downs of fortune; for as the Captain and I were walking on deck, the same evening we left the Commodore, one of the sailors from the round top cried out that he spied a sail on the larboard bow making towards us. Zounds, said the Captain, it is an enemy, and immediately gave orders to clear decks, throw the hencoop overboard and have the Guns in readiness; by the Time this was done, the Enemy, who proved to be an Irish privateer, gave us a

73

furious Broadside; Monsieur de Pivot standing on the quarter deck in 10 or 12 coils of the Cable gave orders with great alacrity and courage. Here I found myself in a miserable plight; for should I seem to act the Coward on the present occasion, my fate would be unavoidably fixed if the Frenchman gained the Victory, but if I fought gallantly I would be treated as a prisoner if the Privateer conquer'd; I therefore resolved to steer a mean between both. Accordingly while the Privateer was at some distance I thought proper to assume an air of fortitude, and afterwards shape my conduct to the day. Now taking off my Wig, I swung it round and gave the men three cheers: Courage my boys! said I, the day is ours. Monsieur de Pivot beholding my bravery extolled me to the very skies and promised me advancement in life according to the services I should perform that day. But now the Cannon of the other ship beginning to rain a shower of Bullets upon us, I thought it most prudent to withdraw, lest my pious resolution should be nipt in the bud by an immature death; so, whispering to the Officer who stood next me that I would just run down into the Cabbin and drink a glass of rum and gunpowder, and come up again courageous and bold as a lion; However, I was not the fool to return so suddenly as I pretended, but waited there, 'till I could learn how the play was going above. In a short time the Irishman bore so hard upon us that the Frenchman gave orders to strike the flag, which I no sooner heard, than I made down thro' a trap door into the hold, and there wrapping myself up in a fishing net, I so entangled myself in it that I seemed to be fast bound like a prisoner. Here I lay struggling and groaning and making most piteous Lamentations, when the Privateer's men came down to search the vessel, and upon seeing me one of them called out to his comrade: Arrah, tear Pryan, here is de Deevil. Oh, no, replied I, in a hoarse hollow voice imitating the Brogue, I am a dear Irish boy, a country man of your own: my name is Pady McFarland, I was taken by these accursed Frenchmen about a week ago, and here tey have kept

74

me in dis vile place, from de blessed light of de sun, moon and stars, widout a drop of drink or a bit of victuals to cross my troat, so dat I am almost starved to deat wid hunger. Ah, dear Pady then, said the Irishman, rise up and come away and by Shaint Patrick, you shall fare as well as the best of us all, for we have taken de Vessel. Oh, my Shewel, quoth I, I might as well fly away wid de ship tro' de air, as to get out of dese ropes wid which I am bound. Arra! my honey; then, said he, I vill cut dem open wid my Gully; this he immediately performed and set me at liberty; pretending to be worn out with famine and ill usage, I clamber'd upon deck upon my hands and feet and saluted the Teagues as deliverers and friends; they indeed treated me very kindly and when the french vessel was ready to be dismissed, for Monsieur de Pivot ransomed her with the same money he received from the Commodore, I say when this was done, I was put aboard the Irish privateer which hoisted sail that very evening and stood away for the north of Ireland. I now entertained them with a relation of my cruel usage aboard the Frenchman. Not a day passed, said I, but I was hauled up to de Halyards to receive four and thirty lashes wid de ropes end. Arra but, said Nees McSwine, the fellow that found me, did you not tell me that you saw neither Sun, moon nor stars de whole time you were a prisoner; I tought by dat you had never been out of de hold at all. Very true, replied I, neither did I see de light of de blessed day, for t'o I was hoisted up on deck dey took care to have my Wig drawn over my face, and braced round my head wid a piece of Tarpaulin, so dat I could neither see nor hear, more dan if I had been at de bottom of de Sea. By this Time Lachland McSwooly the captain coming to see me, asked me where I was born. In Carrickfergus, replied I. Arra my shewel, then, said he, you are a prave Irish poy and if you will go along wid us in de privateering way you shall share in our Fortune and if you are anyting of a scholar you have a chance to be advanced to some office when we return from our cruise. Scholar, said I, I am a profound scholar; I have learned Navigation, Astronomy, Astrology and all de occult sciences wid de greatest attention; I can tell you de names of de twelve constellations in de Zodiac, and de seven planets; I can count you all de stars from de tropics to de Tartric circles and the times of de rising of Orion and de Bear star. The Captain by this time began to stare at me as a prodigy of Learning and immediately all the sailors came crowding about me and listening with their mouths and Ears wide open; for the word had gone out among them, that I was a man of wonderful Scholarship. Yes, Gentlemen, continued I, I have had opportunities of knowing a great deal; I was put to school when I was young to de best masters in de kingdom; I have since travelled tro' de whole vorld; I have conversed wid de persian Mufti, de Bramins of India, de Mandarins of China, de Dervises of Turkey and de Priests of Busiris in Egypt; twas in dis last place I received dis Wig which I now wear and which some of dem told me was made out of de mud of de river Nile; others again said it was de wig Noah wore in de ark and afterwards Shaint Patrick, when he swam from Scotland to Ireland with his head in his teeth. This Staff which I carry in my hand I got from de Pope who told me it was de very staff which de Patriarch Jacob used in his Journey to Padanaram. These books which you see in my wallet are of a religious kind; these, showing them my dictionaries, contain the life of St. Crosten; this, showing my Lucian, is de life of Sht. Patrick. This, pulling out my Xenophon, is a set of Ave Marias in Latin and a copy of Indulgencies which I received from de Pope's own hand. When I had finished my harangue, the Captain treated me with the greatest respect, invited me down to the Cabbin and having supped with him he very politely asked if I was for Bed? I answered in the Affirmative. Patrick O'Connel, said he, conduct this Gentleman to your Birth and lay him down by your messmate Carney McGun, and do you shift for yourself a night. The fellow conducted me to the birth, but went away grumbling and very much displeased to be turned out, and indeed he had a good deal of reason to be so, for, as I afterwards understood, he lay all night in the Coil of a cable rope. This circumstance, small as it may appear, proved the Source of some dreadful accidents; for the Fellow, beyond measure enraged, spared no pains to work my down fall. The first thing he did next day was to signify by nods and whispers that he did not like my appearance. I am much mistaken, said he, if he is not a wizzard, conjuror, or something worse; I was troubled all the night, continued he, with something running up de rope and strange noises in the bow and stern of de ship; and then nodding his head, he seemed to signify that he knew more than he would discover at that time. Hereupon they all began to hint that they had likewise seen something, lest they should seem behind hand in penetration. By my troth, says one, when I got up very early dis morning I saw a Crow on de topmast as big as my head tho' I did not care to speak of it before. Upon my faith, says another, I saw last night two hares run tr'o' de scuttle holes of de ship; I tought den dey were rats, but now I find dey were hares. If dat is de case, says a third, and I verily believe it is, we must take care what we do wid him; last night I saw something on de prow of de ship in de shape of a Woman, which I took to be Sheelah de wife of Neal McCoobory de Cook; now in Trut, I could take my oath it was a witch; but as said, let us take care what we do wid him, for were we to throw him overboard he would blow up a storm which would sink us to de bottom. Ay Faath, and dat's true, replied another, for I remember when old Moll McClonichan wid two or three more witches raised a Whirlwind and carried away an oat-stack of my father's and did much more mischief to de country by Elves shooting de cattle and bewitching de people, 'till Fuccan O'Glaharty shot her wid a pair of silver buttons. Let Donnel O'Loyd immediately then, said they, acquaint de Captain dat de man whom he took for a priest, we have found to be a Wizzard. The Mate having told the Captain the report of the sailors and added a great deal more to it, that he himself had seen me all night up among the shrowds, sometimes handing and reefing the sails and at other times dancing out on the Waves with my Wig in my hand. Egad, said the Captain, if dat is de case, keep a good look out after him and order him not to stir out of de steerage in peril of his Life. I thought it most expedient to obey this command and accordingly kept close. I had however unluckily forgot my wallet on deck and as I dared not venture out for it, the crew resolved to wreck their fury on it, as they were afraid of doing so with me, and likewise thinking they would destroy as much of my power as was concealed in my books. Accordingly they burnt them as I then thought to my unspeakable grief. Here I was obliged to lie in a miserable plight for some days, none daring to come near me to fetch victuals, nor durst I venture out myself. For the Captain had sworn if I did he would shoot me with a silver bullet. In the mean time by long fasting a violent cholic came upon me; I wreathed myself to and fro and groaned most wofully, for indeed I was in extreme misery. The sailors hearing me, fancied I uttered strange and uncouth expressions and were firmly persuaded I was raising the Devil and about this time a fresh Gale springing up, they thought to be sure I was going to destroy the ship. Ay, Fa-ath, says one, now it comes; we'll go to the bottom presently. Something must be done, says another; something must be done. There happened to be an old Priest aboard and it was agreed to call him to put a stop to the impending ruin. The priest coming with a Piggin of holy water threw the half of it down the hatchway upon my face; this I did not regard, as suffering far greater things, but what however gave me some concern was this, that one of the sailors putting down a Fish-gigg, drew up my wig, which shared the same fate with the rest of my things. The storm still increasing, they were terribly scared and began to try every method to get me to lay the storm; when they found nothing would make me do it they hoisted me up with a Tackle and put me into a Tobacco hogshead which the cooper immediately made close and I was tossed into the sea; here I rolled three days and nights and at length found myself at rest on some shore, and knocking out the bung I saw two men coming towards me who I knew by their voices to be Irishmen. Arra, Dear Dennis, says one of them, I'll lay you a groat yonder is a hogshead of Onions or Potatoes from some wreck; by my Troth, says the other, I believe it is. And now being come up, they hoisted up the hogshead on end and concluded it was about half full. Then knocking out the end they saw me sitting very close and taking me for a Wizzard took to the hills; I followed them to some distance endeavouring to persuade them I was a man, but having got up to the mountain they were lost to my view. I now found myself in Ireland, without money, house or home, books to read or a Wig to my head. But the manner in which I behaved and the Adventures which befell me among the wild Irish, shall be the subject of the ensuing chapter.

IL

[Hugh Brackenridge]

Chapter 2ᵈ

Say to what distant regions must I go?
In ev'ry land poor Bombo meets a foe.

When I was fully assured I could not overtake the Irishmen, I made the best of my way over bogs and hills, hoping to find some hospitable place where I might rest my weary head which was now entirely bare for want of a Wig. Thus I travelled near two miles, when being unable to find out the dwelling of any human being, I resolved to return to my hogshead and pass the night there, as in it I had a comfortable nest of straw and hay. When I reached the shore it was almost dark and began to rain; however in I bounced and launching from the shore, I determined to risque the casualties of Fortune, hoping to be driven on some inhabited place. All my provisions were a bushel of potatoes which I had gathered in my excursion after the Irishmen and with these alone I put off to sea; I was immediately borne from the Land by a very rapid current; and shutting my scuttle slept as sound all night as a mouse in a cheese. When the morning came I put my head out and was surprized to see a sloop coming full towards me. As I had no weapons of defence I should certainly have been taken had I not had recourse to a stratagem; for as soon as they came near me and hoisted out the boat to bring me on board, I hallooed with all my might: So ho! by my Troth, I am a Wizzard, as cunning and mischievous as the Devil himself, and if you offer me the least Injury or attempt to fetch me aboard your Yawl I'll raise a storm in an instant and send you all to the bottom. These threats effectually scared them, so that they passed by me in all haste without daring to molest me. After this adventure I bounced about several days, the weather continuing stormy tho' as my cask was tight I had nothing to fear; I was however upon my allowance as to provisions, using no more than four potatoes per Day and having nothing but sea water to drink. The last morning but one that I continued at sea, I opened my scuttle and looking about perceived a box at a distance floating on the water; I therefore in an instant clapped out my paddle and coming up with it, I found it to be close nailed on every side; and as it was no great bulk I hauled it into my Cabbin designing to know the contents of it when I came on shore. The next day I perceived land and towards night found myself at the mouth of a small, tho' navigable, river, up which I was carried by the force of the tide and as it was impossible to stop my career I was drove violently amongst a parcel of sharp headed rocks near the shore and my hogshead being dashed to pieces, I, and my box, were left to shift for ourselves; I immediately clasped it in my arms and swam with all my strength towards the shore, which I at last reached with no other inconvenience than swallowing two or three gallons of salt water; I now looked out for a sharp stone which I soon found and broke open my box with it, which to my great Joy I found to contain my wallet of books and also my red Wig, which the Captain of the privateer had thrown overboard instead of burning them as I imagined. Without multiplying words, I clapped my Wig on my head and threw my wallet over my shoulder and travelled towards a house I saw at a distance, which when I reached, I asked a man who stood by the door, what part of the world I was in; he seemed at first a good deal surprized, but gave me to know that I was in the county of Donnegal and province of Ulster in the NW. part of Ireland; I then asked him the name of the river I was wrecked in; 'tis called in the Irish tongue, answered he, Sough Swilly. The Devil! said I to myself, am I in Ireland yet? Am I never to get out of this cursed place? I then made motion to enter the house, signifying thro' my whole behaviour, that my stomach would feel much better if I had something to eat. The man however did not seem very fond of introducing me, as he had a most cursed scold of a Wife in the house, whose tongue made every thing resound when she let it loose;

but all this could not hinder me from pushing in, which I had no sooner done, than the Dogs and cats about the fire flew at me with most terrible rage and would have torn me into a thousand pieces had I not wielded my staff like a man of courage and resolution so that I layed one Dog dead and maimed a Whippet; one furious cat however stuck in my wig and would not let it go 'till she had brought it together with herself on the floor; I then snatched it up and seizing her by the tail swung her near 10 yards from the house in my fury. The Family and in particular our Scold did not seem much pleased with the havock I made among the domestics of the house, but I not caring three halfpence for any of them took a chair and sitting down by the fire waited impatiently for dinner. At last, my belly prompting me to it, I cryed out, Do you intend to dine here today? Yes, quoth one of them, and what's that to you? What's that to me! replied I, a strange question indeed; why I have lived upon nothing but raw potatoes and salt water these three weeks. Ay! said the man, you have come to a wrong place to pacify your stomach, as we are poor people and have scarcely provisions enough for ourselves. Yet as I see you look very lank, if you will go out into the bog and gather turf for three or four hours, I will bring you something to eat. This proposal I complied with and he sending two or three boys with me to the bogs, I tore up the turf like a Giant so that when he came out with my promised repast, he was really surprized and gave me the victuals chearfully, which I devoured in two or three minutes to my great satisfaction. He then advised me to continue my journey up thro' the country, as he declared I could upon no pretence return to his house, as his wife was resolved to kill me if I once came within gunshot of it; besides, continued he, the people in the inland country are rich and consequently abler to give to beggars, than we who are poor ourselves. Beggars? sir, said I, Zounds do you call me a beggar? Take care what you say. He then begged pardon for his mistake and left me to pursue my Journey thro' the woods; at the end of two days time I came into a well cultivated part of the country full of Inhabitants and houses; I made up to one of them and was kindly received and entertained. Being asked what Countryman I was? an Irishman Faith, by all means, said I. Ay, said the man, and what business do you follow? I am a Schoolmaster, may it please your Worship, said I, I teach all kinds of Languages ancient and modern, all the sciences that are in esteem among the learned. In short there is nothing but what I am perfect master of. Ay, said he, and are you such a remarkable scholar then? In Truth am I, answered I, I understand the Conic Sections. Well, says he, it is a thousand pitys that a person of your knowledge should meet with no preferment in the world. I know of a school among the Wild Irish about 14 miles from here which now is vacant for want of a master; I make no doubt if you are any ways expert in your business, you may get the mastership of it. Arra, my dear, said I, let me alone for dat, I'll lay you a shilling I'll get the possession of it in two days time. Well, said he, I wish you good luck in your Enterprise. Thank you Sir, returned I, and can't we have something to drink on the strength of it. At these words he brought out a bottle of brandy and handing it to me, desired I would name a Toast. Here's a health to brave Ireland, said I, wishing your lands may produce a noble crop of potatoes this Year. After we had drank sufficiently I departed towards my intended school and having arrived at the County of Antrim, wherein it was situated, I enquired for the wild Irish school, and was told I was within a mile of it and ½ a mile of the house of one of the trustees; there I immediately steered my course and when I came to the door, I asked if the Governor of the school was at home. Being answered, Yes, I walked in and desired to see him; I am he, answered an old crooked backed man, and pray what do you want with me? I am a Gentleman, said I, and a schoolmaster; I have heard your school is vacant since the decease of your former master and am come here in order to fill his chair. You have heard very right, said he, and perhaps your design in

83

coming is good, but before you can be promoted to this scholiastical see, you must undergo a strict and accurate examination. Content, said I, and what will you give me by the year? Ten pounds, replied he, has been the salary heretofore, but if we find you anyhow extraordinary you shall have twenty shillings more. Very well, said I, a noble salary; pray let my examination come on quickly; he then sent for the two other trustees, for they were but three in all; and in the meantime, said I, after a person has kept your school three or four years, is there no hopes of any other preferment in Church or state? Ay, ay, quoth he, if you get a black coat, grey wig, put on a demure countenance and throw out scraps of latin heartily you will arrive at the dignity of an Irish priest. Yes, yes, quoth I, I understand you, and what may the living be worth per Annum. Thirty four pounds, said he, but including all the perquisites and presents, it may amount to near thirty seven. Pies and Pigeons, said I, who knows but I may yet be a priest! Very probably, said he, if you behave yourself well. By this time the Trustees were arrived, who excused themselves for their long stay, by being obliged to dig potatoes to send to market next day. Well, said they, is this the gentleman who has proposed to teach the school? Yes, answered I, and I dare say you will be pleased with my abilities. Ay, said they, we shall soon know that, as we are now about to examine you upon Latin, Greek, Anatomy, Philosophy and metaphysics; you must also compose a declamation in our presence, lest if you should do it alone, you might steal out of the books you carry. Never fear that, answered I, I reckon myself as keen a composuist as any in the kingdom; but pray begin to examine me for I am tired waiting for it. Then they hunted about thro' the house for proper books but could find none; then I pulled out my Xenophon and said: Gentlemen here is the life of St. Patrick in Greek, examine me where you please in it. They accordingly took the book and desired me to read off a literal english of the beginning of that Saint's life from the 5th page; this I immediately attempted, but found I could not read a word of the greek as I had quite forgot the characters. Well gentlemen, said I, I am very dim sighted, I wish you would allow me to read the English right off without giving you the trouble to listen to the Greek. This they agreed to and I read as follows. St. Patrick is said to be the son of a certain Gentleman in England, who having spent his youth in Ireland, returned to his native place, and spent the remainder of his life in quality of a Vendue-Master; by all records ancient and modern that are yet extant, he was expert in his business, and sold goods greatly to the advantage of his owners; once however he was detected in a thievish action in endeavouring to steal a gammon of bacon which was for sale. Very well, said they, you are a compleat scholar in Greek, therefore we don't question your abilities in latin. Patrick McSwinney, says one, Examine him on Anatomy. Patrick took the hint and immediately began as follows: How many ribs are there in the human body? Four and twenty on each side, replied I, which by the rules of Arithmetic Artists have found to be fourty eight. Very well, said Patrick. Patrick Mc-Swinney, said Neal O'Bryan, the Gentleman is wrong, he means the Teeth are four and twenty in each jaw, making the sum 48. Arra by my Shoul, don't misunderstand me, I meant to say the teeth. Ay, said McSwinney, and I meant to ask you how many teeth a man has. In the next place, said Patrick, how do you find the Number of nails upon a person? By multiplying means and Extremes together and dividing the quotient by the answer, said I; Very well, said he, and how many do you find them to be? Four and thirty, said I, including the thumb nails. This they agreed was right. And now the next thing in course was Natural Philosophy, which Neal O'Bryan questioned me on thus. What is the End and Design of Philosophy? The end of it is surely to inform our minds and the Design to teach us the knowledge of sublunary things. Very well, said he. What is the reason the Nine planets constantly go round the sun? Because they move in Circles round it. Can you name the Planets? Yes, Mars, Leo, Water-pot, the plow, the harrow, venus and her belts, the Earth and Moon which are both equal to one planet, Job's coffin and the Codfish. Admirably well, said they; there remains nothing now but the Metaphysic, and this Daniel McWigger immediately undertook and began thus: Do you believe you are really a living man and are now standing here before me? Yes, faith, and would I not be a great fool to think otherwise? Ah! this is a bad sign; unless you deny this you can not be admitted to the school. Let us see, answered I, did you not ask me whether I believed I was in Existence? Yes. And what did I answer? You said you did believe it. Oh but Mr. McWigger you misunderstood me, by Sht. Patrick, I meant to say I did not believe I was standing here. Ay, very well, said he, and do you really believe you are nothing but a meer shadow, an immaterial something. Yes, Sir, I verily believe all this as firmly as I do Macnamara's Essay upon childgetting. But, Gentlemen, I hope you will not oblige me to teach this doctrine in the school, for if the boys once got a hint of it they would flog me unmercifully if I were the least harsh towards them. This they agreed to. Patrick McSwinney and Neal O'Bryan said, McWigger, don you think this Gentleman is fit for his promotion? Yes, quo' they, but he has to write his declamation yet. Ay, ay, that's right, said he, here's pen, Ink and Paper, set to it just now. I accordingly scribbled off the following piece on Luxury:

Luxury is that faculty of the human mind whereby we are tempted to eat and drink more than is beneficial to the Stomach; I myself have been guilty of this fault too often, but am determined to reform as soon as I get the quiet possession of my school. But when a person with a voracious Appetite sees any dish desirable to the taste it is a hard matter to refrain from devouring it himself. For my own part I am a great lover of broiled pigeons and turtle doves, not to mention roasted Lamb, Pullets, Capons, Geese, Turkies &c. which I admire exceedingly. I hope Gentlemen if I undertake the management of this school you will supply me with all these utensils, without which I shall have no spirit to carry on matters. There is one thing I forgot to mention and that is, I desire to dine once a week on cold Pork dip'd in Molasses which I love as well as I do my own self. As to Liquor, I expect to be treated constantly with the best kinds, as this will be a main hinge on which the success of my school will turn. That I may be abundantly supplied with all these things is the serious and earnest request of your friend to serve,

Reynardine Bombo

Well done, said Neal O'Bryan, when I had read it aloud to them; the stile is smooth and grand; I perceive your belly is the hero of all your performances of this kind; and I believe so too, said I. Without making many words, I was in a few days established in my school and seated in a large elbow chair like a Justice of the peace, being at the head of near forty scholars; but I found them a pack of untractable fellows incapable of imbibing the good instruction I constantly endeavoured to instill into them. This obliged me to use great severities, whaling them with a rope's end continually and knocking them down with my fists, which so enraged them that at the end of two months they had formed a compleat conspiracy against me, which was executed to my sorrow in the following manner; I came to the school in the morning and continued there with them 'till near night flogging them at the old rate, but now as I was walking backwards and forwards thro' the school, two of them catch'd me by the heels with a cart rope and brought me flat on the ground in a moment; then they all fell upon me and having tied me hand and foot gave me one of the severest drubbings that I have ever had since I saw the light of the blessed day. Then placing me on a Cow they rode me above seven miles across the country thro' bogs and bushes and hauling me down tied my body to a tree and so left me, but as soon as they were gone I pulled out my knife and cutting the rope, set myself at Liberty; then as it was dark,

I laid down upon some turf and took a hearty sleep 'till morning, when not being able to return to the trustees as not knowing the way, I travelled directly forward, passing thro' various inhabited and well cultivated parts, but the people were most remarkably unhospitable, so that from the Time I left my school 'till I reached the NE coast I never had any other bed than the ground or canopy than the sky. When I first saw the sea, I was on a high mountain almost dead for want of food and contemplating my wretched fate; I resolved to leave this rude country and pass over into Scotland where I expected better usage, having a little Scotch blood in my veins. But in the midst of these reflections I composed the following Song on my hard fate and the inhospitality of these wretched Irish:

Sweet are the flowers that crown the vale
And sweet the softly breathing gale
　　That murmurs o'er the hills;
See how the distant lowing throng
Thro' verdant pastures move along
　　Or drink the chrystal rills.

Ah! see in yonder blooming grove
The shepherd tells his tale of love
　　And clasps the wanton fair,
While Winds and trees and shades conspire
To fan the gently burning fire,
　　And banish every care.

But what has love to do with me,
Ill us'd ashore, distress'd at Sea,
　　Now hast'ning to the tomb;
Whilst here I rove and pine and weep
Sav'd from the fury of the deep
　　To find a harder doom.

Ye cruel Fates that guide my ways
And spin too long my hapless days
    Ah draw this scene of strife!
Come fatal sisters from the dead
Prepare to cut the slender thread
    Of my unlucky life.

Expos'd to all the rage and hate
Of ev'ry nation, every state,
    I sigh and weep alone.
Ev'n now the woods and rising grounds
Reecho to the doleful sounds
    And mimic ev'ry groan.

I hate these bow'rs and sweet cascades
That flourish in Hibernian shades;
    The people are unkind;
Regardless of the Pilgrim's fate
They plague my life with scorn and hate
    And give my pray'rs to wind!

Yet shall their guilt in terrors rise
And bring my Ghost before their eyes
    If on this hill I die;
Yes—Witness thou soft gliding flood!
'Tis here I die for want of food,
    This makes my Jaws so dry.

What horror shall possess the breast
Of him that scorns the stranger guest
    And drives him from his door;
Ah, cease my song and oaten flute,
Be thou my voice forever mute
    For I can sing no more.

After I had sung this funeral Dirge over myself I accidentally spyed a tree with apples on, with which I satisfied my stomach, and now having gained a little strength I descended the hill to the sea side, where I saw many fishermen catching Fish in their Nets; as I had a small quantity of money in my wallet, I bought several fish and striking up a fire, I roasted and eat them with great satisfaction; I then traversed the Shore, seeking a passage to Scotland but could get none for sometime.

How I got there and my adventures in that country shall be the subject of the following chapter.

JΓ
[Philip Freneau]

Chapter 3ᵈ

I care no more for Thracia.

ANACREON.

I had not been long on shore when I perceived a sea schooner (coming full sail out of a river) which as they told me was freighted with potatoes for one of the Northern Isles of Scotland. By various methods I at last prevailed upon an Oysterman to put me on board her, whom I rewarded with no other gratuity than bare thanks. As soon as I entered the Vessel, I informed the Captain and Sailors that I had nothing to pay passage but told them if it was agreeable I would serve as Scullion to the Cook 'till we came ashore. This they accepted and I entered immediately upon office. Tho' the passage in good weather is but 24 hours, yet we were, by contrary winds, three days before we arrived at our intended haven in the Island of Mull; here the schooner left me and I was carried in a large Canoo to a port in the Western parts of Scotland which I have now forgot the Name of. To make short of the matter, I shall inform you, that I stayed near two years in the Island of Brittain travelling about doing various kinds of work; one while I was a wool-comber, another time a Waterman; again a Beggar &c., but at the End of this time, I found myself in the Suburbs of the famous and ancient city of London. I stayed here several months, experiencing many surprizing and comical adventures, but I believe by this time you are as tired of hearing my history as I am of relating it; I shall therefore but slightly touch upon the remainder of my adventures and so conclude, I hope to our mutual satisfaction and good liking. To proceed, I took passage in a boat from the river Thames to the port of Dieppe in France; from hence I travelled on foot to the Southern parts of Italy, having suffered much in my long journey by thieves, Robbers and Banditti. But I cannot omit to tell you with what pleasure I traversed the streets of the famous city Rome and how I was struck with admiration at the mighty ruins and superb structures that are scattered up and down this ancient place. Having now arrived at the port of Tarentum, I took shipping for the river Nile in Egypt in quality of Cabbin boy. This voyage brought me very low, and I lay several days at death's door, but happily I recovered in a short time. We sailed up the Nile as far as Memphis and there we landed. I stayed here a few days to view the remarkable curiosities, especially the grand Pyramids situated without the walls, and then prosecuted my Journey with all possible speed towards Mecca. After I had travelled three days alone I was overtook by a Caravan, whom I no sooner had told that I was a Pilgrim going to Mecca on a religious account than they all gave me a hearty welcome, but especially the Pilgrims among them, and mounted me on a Camel so that I travelled at my ease. The only inconvenience worth noticing in this Journey was the want of Water, since for ten days we were confined to a pint per day for ev'ry common man, among whom we Pilgrims were reckoned. In short after six weeks travel we reached Mecca, the place I had so long aimed at. As soon as I arrived I washed my head, hands, and feet, buried my Wig in the Ground and made the best of my way to the mosque, where the body of the famous Mahomet is deposited, and with the most profound respect and adoration laid my dictionaries in one of the most sacred closets of the place. The Caravan stayed here twelve days, which it seems is the limited time. Every morning of these days I prostrated myself on the bare pavement, naked, with my face towards the East, begging the prophet to pardon my crimes and pacify the Ghost of Lucian, an answer to which he returned one night in a vision to my great satisfaction. On the eleventh day of our stay here, as I was returning with a brother Pilgrim from the Mosque, we met a Gentleman, who, hearing me speak english, catched me earnestly by the hand and asked me if I had come there from

England. Yes, Sir, returned I, but am an American born. Bless me! said he, did I ever expect to see a person here from such a distant country! He then insisted upon my staying with him as long as I pleased; I then told him that our Caravan was to set out next morning and I must either go along or be left behind; he then begged I would stay with him 'till it should come back again; but when he could not prevail upon me, he insisted that I should dine with him that day, which I agreed to. His house was very grand and elegant in its appearance and furniture, and he entertained me with the greatest politeness accompanied with wit and good humour. I stayed with him the remainder of the day and at parting he gave me a complete suit of cloaths besides boots, shoes, stockings, hats, overcoats &c. which I should have need of in my Journey; I returned him a thousand thanks and immediately joined the Caravan which left the city by sunrise. But what Joy did I feel! when I found myself returning to my native Country provided with cloaths and other necessaries which made me look more like a human creature than I did before. We met with nothing very remarkable in the way except once, that a furious band of Bedouin Arabians set upon us, but we handled our arms so well that they were repulsed with loss. At last we arrived at Alexandria, where I found a ship sailing for Cadiz in Spain; I instantly put my baggage aboard, being enabled to pay my passage by the bounty of the Gentleman of Mecca. After a prosperous voyage we arrived safely at old Spain, where I left the Alexandrian vessel and travell'd on horseback in Company with several merchants to the City of Lisbon, the Capital of Portugal. Here I found a ship bound for Philadelphia laden with wines and ready to sail; I immediately got aboard and in less than two hours got out of the river Tagus, with a fair wind. In our way home we touched at the Island of Madeira, where I was invited ashore by several European and American merchants, who used me with the greatest humanity and kindness and, when our ship sailed, dismissed me with several very valuable presents.

93

We now weighed Anchor and left this delightful Island, which is incommoded with nothing, but the Terrors of that Diabolical and pernicious court of Inquisition which reigns here with all imaginable fury. On the fourth day of our departure, we were attacked by a prodigious storm, which raged with unremitted fury for several days and drove us a great way out of our intended course. But at last the storm began to abate, and a favourable gale sprang up, which in three days brought us into the well known capes of Delaware, and in about eight and forty hours we anchored at the flourishing city of Philadelphia. Here I stayed several days and was gladly entertained by several gentlemen who had formerly been of my acquaintance. I now began to think of returning to the ancient castle where I had formerly spent the most agreeable part of my life, and accordingly by means of a Stage waggon I arrived in the Evening at a place I had been absent from so long a time and in which I had experienced so many surprizing adventures, the one half of which I have not set down for fear of tiring your patience. Experience has taught me to be wise and leave the paths of folly for those of Virtue and Wisdom. I have passed thro' high and low life. In me you have seen the Sage, the Beggar, the Droll, the Gentleman, and what not? I now conclude the history of my own life even 'till this moment and I now inform everybody that I intend to pass the remainder of my life in peace and Ease, pursuing the most sublime and noble studies, that I may hereafter inform and instruct the world both by precept and Example.

JΓ

[Philip Freneau]

The End of the Sage Bombo's relation.

The Conclusion of
Mr. Bombo's Life.

Ah! coulds't thou break thro' fate's severe decree
Another Bombo should arise in thee.

V<small>IRG</small>.

Mr. Bombo according to his pious resolution of retiring from the noise and hurry of the world betook himself to his chamber and spent the chief part of his time in perusing various Authors of the Philosophic and the moral kind, whose sentiments joined with his own made him the most perfect scholar of his Age. At length growing weary with the perpetual noise and hurry of the Castle he retired to a pleasant country seat on the banks of Stony Brook about 16 furlongs from the castle. And here he spent his time till he arrived at an extreme old age, which sensibly diminished his stature and turned his locks grey, and indeed I verily believe the good old man would have turned into a Whipperwill or Grasshopper as the fabled Tithonus of old, had not death, for which he had long waited, put a speedy end to all his travels, cares, crimes and comical adventures. This last scene of his days was very affecting but I shall forbear to transmit it to Posterity, as the same tragedy must be acted over again as long as the world stands and so no one can be ignorant of it. He left all his estate consisting of books, papers, Manuscripts &c. to his friends and Executors Mr. John Smith of N. England and Mr. Joshua Hart, both residing in the Castle, who it is expected will one day oblige the world with a publication of his Lucubrations both in prose and verse founded upon various Moral, Philosophic and comical subjects. He ordered in his last will that he should be buried in a pleasant wood under a tall beech, by the side of a gentle stream about half a mile from the Castle; this injunction I am informed his executors complied with and over his tomb placed a large flat stone having the following Epitaph engraved on it at large:

> HIC JACET corpus viri venerandi
> Reynardini Bombo:
> Qui, multis itineribus laborisque peractis;
> Vita decessit ad villam Amabilem,
> Ripis fluvii lapidori, sitam;
> Ætatis sua XCVIII.

> Ab omnibus bonis
> In vita dilectus,
> Et in morte deploratus:
> Hic, Viator! Hic, lachrymas Effunde.
> Hic fungeto inani munere
> Et lugeto Virum fortem, generosum, doctumque.

This inscription was composed by his learned and ingenious friend and countryman Mr. Nathan Perkins who has since that time followed his friend. But tho' it is actually affirmed by some, that this Epitaph was engraved in large capital letters on the stone; yet the writer of this chapter declares that tho' he searched every spot and hillock in this wood he has never yet been able to find our Pilgrim's tomb, tomb-stone or inscription, tho' very probably the Autumnal leaves falling has obscured it from sight. Should any person be so happy as to discover it, I would desire him to get the following lines engraved under the latin Epitaph:

> Renowned shade, whose happy doom
> Consigns thee to a rural tomb,
> Here slumb'ring let thy golden dreams
> Pervade the woods and gliding streams,
> While in the dark and gloomy shade
> Around thee weeps each Sylvan maid.
> The morning comes; the vocal throng
> For thee begin their mournful song;

The Muses round thy silent hearse
Forever chaunt the noble verse,
Whose tragic strains at nightly noon,
From heav'n can draw the lab'ring moon,
Make loftiest forests lend an ear
And angels lean from heav'n to hear.

But what does it signify to crowd his tomb with Epitaphs? His travels so remarkably eventful have raised him a monument more noble than any material one whatever, which would be subject to the injuries of Time and misfortunes. We therefore conclude our history, hoping that no one hereafter will attempt or presume to say, that they intend to raise up the bones of Father Bombo and carry him in romance to distant countries; and also let no person be so bold as to write any second or third parts to this history, as we now declare it is completed as much as it ever will be. Our sage hero has undergone toils sufficient to kill any common man and we now leave him to take his chance, either to fly on the wings of fame, or sink in eternal obscurity. Finis.

JΓ
[Philip Freneau]